FLOWERS FROM THE GARDEN

Flower Arranging Made Easy

LEILA AITKEN

BBC BOOKS

AUTHOR'S NOTE

I should like to thank Lilias Hoskins for her expert teaching and unstinting advice with this book. Also my husband, Robbie, for his readiness to help in any way and not minding about the food (there wasn't a lot) and the stour (there was).
This book is dedicated, with love, to my family, especially Big Granny and Little Granny.

Published by BBC Books,
a division of BBC Enterprises Limited,
Woodlands, 80 Wood Lane, London W12 0TT
First published 1990

ISBN 0 563 36025 9

Set in 11/13pt Janson by Ace Filmsetting Ltd, Frome

Printed and bound in Great Britain by Redwood Press Ltd, Melksham
Colour separations by Dot Gradations Ltd, Chelmsford
Cover printed by Richard Clay Ltd, Norwich

CONTENTS

Foreword by Lilias Hoskins

Foreword

This book is designed to inspire and encourage anyone with an interest in flower arranging. Starting with the simpler designs for the beginner, it continues on to the more elaborate designs using much more plant material. By following the simple and basic instructions in this book, in conjunction with the television series you should be capable of producing a number of pleasing designs suitable for all types of settings and occasions, ranging from a simple jug of roses, to a large pedestal design. The latter design is most useful for anyone involved in arranging their church flowers.

Over the years designs have evolved to suit our life styles and the settings into which the flowers will be placed. Recently, designs from the Continent have been appearing more and more, particularly in our florists' shops. Whatever the style, they all have their own particular charm and interest. They create a talking point at a dinner party, add a touch of colour to any room, cheer a patient in hospital, show sympathy at a time of sadness, show affection to a loved one, or beautify a church.

Nowadays a garden is not necessary, as flowers and foliage can be bought not only from the traditional flower shops, but even from the local garage, and of course they can become part of your weekly shop as more and more supermarkets are stocking a very good selection of cut flowers. This means we can all be flower arrangers.

For the past three decades flower arrangement has increased in popularity. There are many thousands of flower club members the length and breadth of Great Britain. There are 10 000 members in Scotland alone.

As with most hobbies, flower arranging is a skill which can be improved upon as the years go by, with classes being held by floral art clubs and local authorities. For those wishing to go a step further, a three-year course is organised by City and Guilds

London, and run at various colleges throughout the country.

Most flower clubs are affiliated to the National Association of Flower Arrangement Societies, NAFAS for short. This is the governing body of the flower arrangement movement in Great Britain. Its aim is to nurture and foster the love of plant material, and to uphold the laws of conservation.

Through an interest in flowers many friendships are made. In twenty-five years of flower arranging, I have found it an absorbing hobby to the point of becoming an obsession. Most of all it is the fun and friendship engendered by this delightful hobby which I appreciate. I hope this book will encourage you to become involved in the art of flower arranging and gain from it as much pleasure as I have.

Lilias Hoskins is Vice-chairman of the Scottish Association of Flower Arrangement Societies. She is a demonstrator, judge and teacher of the City and Guilds' Flower Arrangement Course and has won many awards for her floral arrangements.

BEGINNING FLOWER ARRANGING

1
Why Arrange Flowers?

Why bother? Do you really need to arrange flowers? The beauty of any flower is obvious. Won't any 'arrangement' make them look stiff and contrived? And people say, 'Oh, I don't agree with flower arrangement. I like flowers the way they are.' Perhaps the people who say this only say it because they can't arrange flowers and don't really want to learn!

Anyway, try this with a simple bunch of chrysanthemums—those sprays of chrysanths which can be bought from florists and supermarkets all year round. Just put them in a vase the way they are. Wherever you place them in the home, the most noticeable part of these flowers is the stalk, and in a week or so it will be the withering leaves!

Now get a small cereal bowl and a square of oasis. If you haven't heard of oasis before, see page 12. Soak the oasis and

Just put them in a vase the way they are

wedge it into the bowl. A square of oasis in a round bowl allows space to add water. Divide up the stalks on the stem of chrysanths, one head to a stalk. They will be of unequal lengths, which is exactly what you want. And remove all the leaves because they usually die before the flowers.

Now go out and pick four or five short sprays of golden privet (*Ligustrum ovalifolium* 'Aureo-marginatum') from a hedge, roughly the same unequal lengths as the flowers. Also, pick some similar lengths of lady's mantle (*Alchemilla mollis*), the soft yellow-green fluffy flower, with serrated edges to its leaves, that grows like a weed in some gardens.

Start with the foliage. Insert the privet into the oasis with all the stem ends pointing to the centre of the bowl but coming in from different angles, upwards as well as downwards. Add the lady's mantle throughout the privet and finally add the chrysanthemums, facing in different directions.

You can now look into the face of each individual flower, framed in an outline of greenery. If you compare the two arrangements of chrysanthemums, which one do you prefer, and which brings out the full beauty of the flowers?

9

The flowers should face in different directions

Making a simple posy of flowers like this not only illustrates the need to arrange flowers in such a way so as to show them to advantage and make them last, but it also underlines the difference between flower arranging and floristry, which are two distinct ways of treating flowers.

Flower arranging is the art of creating pictures with flowers, for your own satisfaction and relaxation and so that other people can appreciate and enjoy the flowers more fully. It uses as much and, usually, more, foliage than flowers. This is one reason why flower arrangers are often keen gardeners.

Floristry is an art and a business, concerned primarily with the commercial aspects of packaging and presenting flowers to the public as attractively as possible. It uses mostly flowers, with very little greenery. Often these are grouped as a sheaf, for the recipient to arrange. Flowers can also be bought ready-arranged, in bouquets, baskets or pots. Floristry sometimes uses specialised techniques which are not needed for flower arranging, such as wiring, for which training and skill are needed. If you try wiring flowers for a corsage, you will appreciate just how much skill is needed.

Because many aspects of floristry and flower arranging overlap, your florist can be a great help to you. Both arts require an appreciation of colour and form, and an eye for combining the two. But the big bonus of flower arranging is that you only have to satisfy yourself!

Fashions and styles in flower arrangement change over time and vary from country to country. The most popular arrangements in Britain at the moment are loose, mass country-style designs, with flowing lines made to look natural and uncontrived. Modern and abstract styles enjoy less of a following.

You cannot adopt or copy any style of floral art without first understanding the basic principles of flower arrangment in both line and mass arrangements. You need to know how to follow a direction or line with each flower or piece of foliage you place; how to combine the various forms and colours of plant material, and how to cut them to different lengths in relation to each other and to the container, in order to create a balanced and harmonious whole.

The best way to learn is to start with simple line arrangements, which you can then fill out with more plant material, building up to more elaborate designs and finally to large mass and pedestal arrangements. Work your way systematically through this book. Gradually you will absorb the basic guidelines for arranging flowers and begin to develop your own preferences and style. You need to practise with as many sizes and types of flower arrangement as you can. Offer to do flowers for friends and for the local church. Join a flower club or evening class, and go to see flower arranging demonstrations. You will always learn something new.

Always keep in mind that flower arranging is a joy. It should be hugely satisfying, using flowers to create a picture, however transient. Flower arranging is about tranquillity, creativity and relaxation. To be absorbed in creating anything, whether it is a flower arrangement, a sculpture or a piece of needlework, makes for contentment. When *you* like the finished arrangement and it gives *you* pleasure, and when you feel sufficiently confident with your efforts to present arranged flowers as gifts, then you are well on the way to becoming a proficient flower arranger.

2
Learning to Arrange Flowers

What will you need? Initially, you will not need to spend much money on extra equipment to practise the art of arranging flowers. The one thing you must have is a supply of floral foam, commonly known by its trade name of Oasis.

This is a water-retaining plastic foam, which is wedged or taped into the flower container and for a beginner it is essential. If you haven't used it before, you will be pleasantly surprised at just how easy it makes the task of positioning the flower stems exactly as you want them. It is available in different-sized blocks or shapes from florists, department stores and garden centres. The most economical way is to buy large blocks and cut them to the exact size and shape you need with a sharp kitchen knife. Buy several blocks at a time so that you always have it available.

The oasis must be soaked thoroughly in a bucket or large bowl of water before placing in the container. A 50 g (2 oz) piece of oasis will weigh 2 kg (4 lb) after it has been immersed for about 10 minutes. It is ready for use when the block sinks to the level of the water. Although a few flower stems, such as anemones and narcissi, do not like being inserted into oasis, most flowers thrive and last well in it. Oasis can be re-used until it is so full of holes it disintegrates, and you can turn a thick block upside-down and use the underneath. It cannot be re-used satisfactorily once it has dried out, so if you are not re-using a soaked block at once, always store it in a sealed plastic bag.

If you are a real beginner, go out and buy some oasis and a bunch of roses, plus some foliage. Or, if you can, cut seven or more garden roses at different stages of development: some in bud and some full blown. And try this. Find a large jug or tankard. Cut the oasis so that it will wedge firmly into the container, with a gap for topping up with water, and leave 5–7.5 cm (2–3 in) showing above the rim. This is important. Always cut oasis so that it is higher than the rim of the container. You can then place the flower stems to flow downwards and curve gracefully. Soak the oasis as instructed above and then wedge it into the container.

Cut the smallest bloom or bud so that the length of the stem is about one-and-a-half times the height of the container. Now imagine a point right at the heart of the protruding part of the oasis, and insert the rose with the tip of the stem pointing downwards towards that point.

Imagine a central point in the oasis

That is the longest rose. Cut the next rose slightly shorter and insert it from the side, horizontally into the oasis, also pointing it to the centre. Cut the next rose shorter still and insert it from below the rim of the tankard, in an upwards direction, again pointing to the centre of the oasis.

Repeat this with all the roses, trying not to line them up. Cut each rose to a slightly different length and place in a different plane. The largest roses should have the shortest stems and be placed near the centre, to form the focal point of the arrangement. Fill in the gaps between the flowers and hide the oasis with the foliage off-cuts from the stems. (See illustration in colour section.)

Not only have you now learnt how to use oasis but you will incidentally have learnt one of the basic guidelines of flower arranging: each flower should be in isolation so that the beauty of individual blooms can be appreciated and enjoyed.

What other equipment will you need? By now you will have realised that you need scissors. Special florist's scissors with short blades are available from florist's suppliers or garden centres. Small secateurs are also useful for woody stems, such as those of roses.

You will also need green florist's tape to hold the oasis in place in some containers. Small, cheap, plastic 'frogs' will hold the oasis when it cannot be wedged firmly, and a very sticky substance, like green plasticine, is sold by the inch to fasten down the frogs. Buy some large-mesh chicken wire, which is scrumpled loosely to hold flower stems; reel wire and florist's stub wires to strengthen weak stems; wire cutters; a sharp knife; a selection of flower buckets and a small plant-sprayer. None of these items is expensive and you can get them all from a florist or garden centre. It is a good idea to keep all your basic equipment together in a large tin or plastic box.

I haven't mentioned pin holders, which are small, round, lead bases with vertical pins, because they are expensive. To begin with, you will not need one, but eventually you may want to use them for holding branches and thick flower stems in certain types of arrangement.

All this equipment, sometimes known as the mechanics of flower arranging, is there to anchor the flowers securely and to enable you to place them in such a way that the finished arrangement looks uncontrived, loose and natural. The mechanics are an integral part of flower arranging but should never, ever be seen! In other words, you are going to all this trouble to make a secure foundation which should make the blooms look almost as though they have grown there naturally.

3
Choosing a Container

The one thing you will *not* need for arranging your flowers is a flower vase—the conventional type that is. A flower vase produced the result you see on page 9. You *will* need a selection of different containers in varying shapes, heights, weights and textures, ranging from a smooth, flat dish, to a rough, concrete urn. Baskets, ceramic and unglazed pottery jugs and bowls, wooden boxes, copper kettles, pewter mugs, shells, antique china bowls, teapots, candlesticks, figurines, lamp bases, pie dishes and cake stands are all valuable containers for arranging flowers.

Although almost anything can be used as a flower container, what you put your flowers in is a vital part of your finished arrangement. The container should blend sympathetically with the flowers to make a pleasing overall picture. It should not dominate, nor be the first thing in the arrangement to catch the eye. Think carefully about your choice of container.

Does it harmonise with the flowers? A brown pottery jug, for example, is perfect for strong orange marigolds, but would be quite wrong for the delicacy of lily-of-the-valley, which would be enhanced by a crystal goblet.

Is the colour appropriate? A stark white container often dominates the arrangement and is the first thing to attract the eye, detracting from all but white flowers. Matt black, dull green, earth brown and the muted sheens of copper and brass are all more complementary to most flowers and foliage.

Is the weight and scale of the container appropriate for the type of flower? The huge shaggy heads of chrysanthemums, for instance, would balance both in weight and scale in a terracotta urn, but would appear out of scale and unstable in a slender silver pedestal, and top heavy in a small, squat container.

Are the textures of the flowers, foliage and container in harmony?
The rough, feathery texture of dried flowers, for example, will
harmonise with rustic basketwork, but would be dominated by
the smooth glossiness of an enamelled bowl.

Is the container suitable for the setting? The type of room and the
occasion should have some bearing on your choice of container. A modern, square, black vase will look out of place in a
Victorian-style drawing room, but is ideal in a contemporary
setting.

You don't need to spend large sums of money on containers.
Most flower arrangers enjoy searching in junk shops, at antique
fairs and even in rubbish skips, and putting imagination to
work on old teapots and lamp bases. If you see a pair of legs
sticking out of a roadside skip, you can be sure they belong to a
flower arranger! Most garages sell off at a reduced price cans of
discontinued colours of car spray paint, with which you can
transform unpromising objects or cheap plastic pots into
gleaming containers in black, gold, green or even antique
bronze.

4
Conditioning Flowers and Foliage

Although I am very loath to burden you at the outset with the technicalities of flower arranging, the conditioning of flowers and foliage you use is very important. However, if you are fired with enthusiasm to try out an arrangement, skip this chapter for now and come back to it when you can study it over a cup of coffee.

Conditioning flowers makes them last a few days more, so you can enjoy your handiwork for a longer time. It is basically a process of making sure that the foliage and flowers are able to take up water efficiently and stay in good condition.

If you have bought a bunch of flowers that wilted almost as soon as you brought them home, which occurs frequently with roses, the florist may not be at fault. What happens is that as soon as a stem end is cut, air rushes in. When the stem is out of water, the cut end begins to 'heal' and forms a callus during transit, sometimes with an air lock behind, so the plant cannot drink water and wilts.

The first step in conditioning all flowers and foliage is to re-cut the stem ends, under water if possible, and to put all plant material straight into a bucket of water. Cut the stem ends on a slant, to maximise water intake, and also because a straight end may seal against the base of the bucket, preventing the uptake of water. After re-cutting, some plants require further conditioning, which varies according to the type of stem.

Soft stems, such as those of lilies, should stand in water in a cool place for a minimum of two hours. The stems should fill with water and feel stiff.

Hard, woody stems, such as those of roses, need the ends split. Cut with secateurs or hammer the ends. After splitting, arrange with the stem ends level, wrap the heads loosely in a plastic bag for protection and hold the ends in 2.5 cm (1 in) of boiling water for approximately 15 seconds. Then leave them to condition in water, as for soft stems. After a very short time most wilted rosebuds will revive.

Milky stems, such as those of euphorbias and poppies, exude a milky, latex-like fluid, which can cause skin irritation and kill other flowers. To prevent the sap leaking out, seal the ends over a candle or gas flame. Stand them in water, as for soft stems.

Hollow stems, such as those of lupins, hollyhocks (*Althaea*) and delphiniums, need to be filled with water to last well. Turn the flower upside down and pour in water from a small spout, or use a funnel. Plug the end with cotton wool, which will help to draw water up the stem.

There are other additional procedures which help certain plants and foliage.

Lilac (*Syringa*), mock orange (*Philadelphus*) and clematis Remove all the foliage to make the flowers last. Then give them the boiling water treatment, as for hard, woody stems.

Chrysanthemums Remove all the foliage, except that closest to the flowers, to help prevent slime and bacteria growing in the water. A few drops of household bleach added to the water will also help to prevent this.

Tulips, iris and ranunculus Wrap tightly in newspaper before putting in water to condition, as the paper will keep the stems straight. Tulips in particular tend to grow after they have been cut and, if unrestrained, will grow in all directions.

Violets, hydrangea and clematis heads The easiest way is to float these on water, rather than stand them in it to condition. It gives a greater surface area to absorb the water. The hydrangea heads can even be submerged upside down in the water for up to two hours.

Mimosa Condition with an airtight plastic bag over the flowers to maintain humidity around them. Mimosa will not last long in a dry atmosphere as the pollen dries out quickly and sheds. Arranging it in warm water will increase the humidity around the flowers.

Pinks and carnations Cut just above a node and condition them in lemonade or in a sugar solution of 1 tsp sugar dissolved in each 600 ml (1 pt) water.

Mature foliage Immerse completely in water for at least two hours to condition it, as some water is absorbed through the leaves. The exception is grey foliage, which should not be submerged as it loses its bloom and becomes water-logged. Evergeen foliage benefits from a swirl in soapy water.

Always remove any foliage that will be below the water line in an arrangement, otherwise it encourages bacteria to grow, which in turn shortens the life of the flowers.

Immature foliage Give all immature foliage and single large leaves the boiling water treatment as for hard, woody stems. Half a soluble aspirin dissolved in the arranging water also helps by closing the pores of the leaves and preventing loss of moisture.

Autumn foliage This is lovely to use in the shades of gold and brown. It will last longer if sprayed with a solution of one part glycerine to three parts warm water to coat the leaves and prevent them from drying out further.

5
The Principles of Design

Many people instinctively appreciate good art form, whether in painting, sculpture, wood carving or flower arrangement. But when you try to analyse what it is that makes a work of art satisfying and pleasing to the eye, you come across words like balance, proportion, scale, rhythm, contrast, dominance and harmony. These are known as the principles of design.

A good flower arranger unconsciously fulfils all the principles of design without putting them into words. As you become proficient in arranging flowers, you too will instinctively fulfil them. But until then, this brief explanation of the principles of good design which are common to all art will help you to understand what exactly it is you are trying to achieve.

Balance in flower arranging means visual as well as physical balance. The flowers must not look as though they are ready to fall over in too delicate a pot, nor should they look insignificant in an over-large container. An arrangement may be perfectly stable, but if it appears top heavy, it will be upsetting to the onlooker. If it is bottom heavy, the flowers may be overlooked in favour of the container. A well balanced arrangement should be soothing and restful to the eye.

Proportion concerns the quantity of flowers in relation to the bulk of the container. Proportion and balance are obviously inter-dependent: when the amount and size of the flowers in relation to the shape and size of the container are correct, then the arrangement is balanced and visually satisfying.

The scale of each flower in relation to its neighbour is also important. Large, shaggy heads of chrysanthemums, for example, will look wrong next to delicate sweet peas (*Lathyrus*) or dainty pinks, because the scales are so different, and the design is somehow uneasy on the eye. However, if you include an intermediate-sized flower, such as large single carnations, then the three types will be graded in size and related in scale. (This is called transition.)

Lack of movement or rhythm in a design is illustrated by the static appearance of an arrangement composed only of one type of spray chrysanthemum. It lacks interest, and the arrangement is monotonous, because of the uniformity of size and colour. But add some mixed freesias and the display comes to life because of the contrast in the shape, colour and texture of the flowers. Using curving plant material and arranging it to flow through a design in a rhythmic sequence also gives movement and vitality.

An arrangement may lack interest if there is no centre, no dominant flowers or leaves, to catch the eye. Place the largest flowers or leaves in the centre of a design to give it a focal area and make it more satisfying.

Harmony is achieved when all the above conditions are fulfilled. A harmonious design looks balanced because the proportion of flowers to container is correct; the size of plant material is related in scale and colour; and the arrangement looks comfortable in its surroundings and suits the room and the occasion.

Some people have an instinctive knowledge of these principles of design, and without analysing it, can create arrangements which fulfil these criteria. Other people are greatly helped by being able to reason it out and see the principles behind all good design. Even a little understanding of these principles makes flower arranging that much simpler. You will be able to create a picture with flowers which satisfies your own artistic sense. It also means you can criticise your own work, and when it does not satisfy you, analyse it to find out why.

In an attempt to turn this theory into practical instruction, Chapter 7 sets out twelve guidelines which should help the beginner. Always remember that these are not rigid rules. They are merely suggestions to give you confidence in flower arranging until you develop your own style.

Choosing a container for an arrangement is discussed on page 15.

6
The Elements of Design

In trying to explain the principles underlying good design, several other significant words have cropped up—form, texture, colour and space. Whereas the principles of design are abstract, something you create yourself, the elements of design are the 'bricks' with which you build.

Form is the three-dimensional shape of the material used. Flower arrangers simplify these shapes by calling them lines, points and transitional, in-between or intermediate shapes. The most pleasing arrangements usually include all three.

Texture is the touchable quality of the material selected. Sameness of texture makes for monotony in a design—a basket of dried flowers is one example, whereas contrasts in texture add vitality. Flower arrangers are concerned primarily with visual texture.

Colour is the most important element in flower arranging. To begin with you will find that you select flowers in your favourite colours. It is important to give some thought to developing your colour sense, so that you can happily mix and match the colours of all plant material. When thinking of ideas for colour schemes, study a colour wheel in an art book. It may seem complicated, until you realise that it is simply the rainbow, incorporated in a circle, with all the colours that blend well together placed next to each other.

At the outset you will want to decide on the colour scheme for your arrangement. You may choose to match the furnishings of a room or the colour of a dinner service. For example, your colour scheme may be cream and yellow. You then choose your main flower, perhaps the rose 'Peace'. Your choice of colours for the companion flowers is then dictated by 'Peace'. Pink alstroemeria and pale yellow spray carnations will echo the colours in the petals of the rose. Obviously, with a delicate colour scheme like this, you would not choose dark strident foliage which would dominate the flowers. Pale green and soft grey foliage would enhance the flowers best.

You can either choose to make a wonderful polychromatic display with flowers of every hue, or to be selective with a more sophisticated scheme with fewer colours or shades of a single colour.

Using flowers in various shades of one colour is known as a monochromatic colour scheme. When you start to collect flowers and foliage together for such an arrangement you realise you cannot literally make an arrangement of one hue (pure colour), because there are so many shades, tints and tones in every individual flower.

Bold, striking arrangements can be made by using complementary colours—those directly opposite each other on the colour wheel. Red carnations with dark green holly are one example, as is the simple but very pleasing arrangement of orange marigolds in a bright blue pot.

Arrangements which use colours next to each other on the colour wheel are easy and satisfying to create and are known as adjacent or analogous schemes. Orange and yellow chrysanthemums with bright green beech leaves in a copper container are a delightful example. At the other side of the colour wheel is a mixture of mauve, red and blue anemones in a grey clay pot.

Colour is a vast subject, and the best way to study it in depth is from art books. But the flower arranger should be aware of the following properties of colour which can affect an arrangement.

Colours such as purple, dark red and blue appear to recede. Others, such as orange, yellow and white, appear to advance. So if you mix purple and yellow in a church display which will be seen from a distance, the purple ones will look like holes in the arrangement. Dark flowers are also dominant and have more visual weight. Place them low down or towards the centre in a design, to avoid creating a top heavy effect. A colour, especially a dominant one, should be repeated either in a flowing line or in a group, creating rhythm. Dotting colours through a design makes for confusion.

Space in flower arranging may not be tangible, but it plays a very important part by defining an arrangement or an individual flower. In the way that a house is enhanced by the space of a large garden and diminished by being crowded next to its neighbour, or a picture is defined by the space within the frame, so a flower arrangement is enhanced by the use of space.

Space has very positive qualities. It can make all the difference between an arrangement that is crowded and unsatisfying, and one that is restful to the eye. Space can also change a design completely. Any arrangement on a pedestal has an added feeling of lightness, as the space below the pedestal is a visual part of the design. Some modern and abstract flower arrangements use fewer flowers and make essential use of space, particularly enclosed space, as in this modern design, entitled 'Love in a Mist', which uses silvered foliage and a single flower on a slate base.

A modern design illustrating the use of enclosed space

7
Twelve Guidelines for the Flower Arranger

1 Measure the height of the container. The highest point of the arrangement should be approximately one and a half times the height of the container. If you are using a container which is wider than it is tall, the highest point should be one and a half times the width.

2 All plant material should radiate from a central point, and stems should never cross. Imagine a point inside the oasis and insert all the stems towards it. This makes the arrangement look natural and uncontrived.

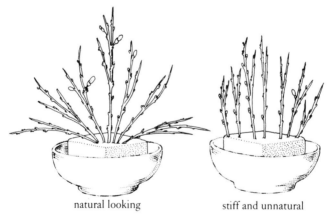

natural looking   stiff and unnatural

Plant stems should radiate from a central point

3 Select a minimum of three types of foliage: line foliage for the shape, such as broom (*Cytisus*), phormium, privet (*Ligustrum*) or stephanandra; large leaves such as bergenia, hosta, *Fatsia japonica*, alchemilla or magnolia; intermediate, transitional or 'fussier' foliage with either smaller leaves or different-shaped leaves, such as escallonia, cotoneaster, choisya or skimmia.

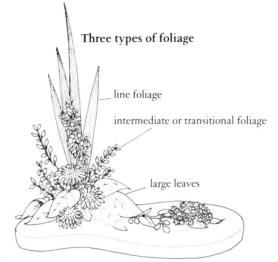

Three types of foliage

line foliage

intermediate or transitional foliage

large leaves

4 Vary both the colours and the textures of the foliage. The woolly grey of *Senecio greyi*, for example, will contrast well with the lime-green of *Elaeagnus* 'Limelight' or with the bronze *Tellima grandiflora* 'Purpurea'. However, don't use too much variegated foliage or too many different types in one arrangement, as this confuses the arrangement and the arranger.

5 Complete the outline of the design with the foliage first and then add the flowers. The tallest foliage stem should be inserted approximately two-thirds of the way towards the back of the oasis and lean slightly backwards. Several shorter stems should be added behind it, pointing in the same direction, to avoid a thin, one-dimensional look.

6 Select flowers in various stages of development—buds, half-open blooms and fully-open flowers. Combine the different floral shapes: the upright, spiky forms, such as delphinium, crocosmia, gladioli, polygonatum, freesia and tellima; round, open-faced forms, such as chrysanthemum, scabious, gerbera and rose; intermediate forms, such as spray carnation. *Alchemilla mollis* (lady's mantle), sweet pea, alstroemeria and nicotiana.

7 Place the flowers in the arrangement so that they are graded in size, with the largest or most dominant flowers to the centre of the design, the buds and smallest flowers to the outside and tips of the arrangement, and the intermediate sizes filling in.

8 Flowers should be cut to different lengths, so that no two flowers of the same length are next to each other.

9 Some of the flowers should always be recessed, with some 'in', some 'out'. This avoids the flat, static look with all flowers on the same level. Do not have all the flowers facing the front; some should turn sideways, as they do naturally.

10 Always have some foliage or flowers curving over the front of the container to break the hard line of the lip and unify the plant and non-plant material.

11 Each flower should be seen in isolation in its own space and not touching its neighbour. Never overcrowd an arrangement; as the saying goes, 'Leave room for the butterflies'.

12 Create a focal point for the eye to rest on in the design either with the largest and most dominant flower, or by using large leaves or the strongest colour towards the centre.

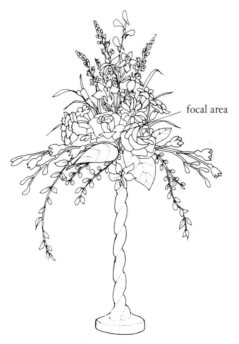

focal area

Create a focal area for the eye to rest on

8
Plants to Grow for Flower Arranging

You will want to grow plants especially for your flower arrangements. Creating an all-foliage design will not only make you more aware of the variations in the shapes of leaves, the subtle shadings of colour and differences in texture, but you will begin to appreciate how these variations add interest and vitality to an arrangement. You will soon realise the gaps in your own garden and the types of foliage you lack.

You need a mixture of *all* colours of foliage, green, lime-green, variegated foliage, grey, silver, red and bronze. You also need to bear in mind the three forms basic to flower arrangement: strong 'line' foliage to make the outline; smaller-leafed, bushier 'fillers'; and the large leaves needed at the centre of the arrangement to give depth. Make sure your garden has a selection of each of these forms as well as trailing foliages such as *Vinca* (periwinkle) and *Lonicera* (honeysuckle). You will develop your own favourites, but below are some of mine, roughly grouped as the categories overlap. Some can be used for both outline and fillers or as fillers and trailers, and some, like variegated ivy, are indispensable to give lightness in any design.

Outline foliage: *Fagus* (beech); *Phormium tenax* (New Zealand flax), both forms—dull grey-green and variegated; *Cytisus* (broom); *Crocosmia*; *Pittosporum*; *Ligustrum ovalifolium* 'Aureo-marginatum' (golden privet); *Weigela florida* 'Variegata'; *Stephanandra tanakae*; *Cotoneaster franchetii*; *Berberis thunbergii* 'Atropurpurea'; *Elaeagnus pungens* 'Maculata'; *Eucalyptus gunnii*; *Rosmarinus officinalis*; *Rosa rubrifolia*.

Filler foliage: *Escallonia*; *Berberis*; *Choisya ternata*, also its golden form—'Sundance'; *Skimmia japonica*; *Mahonia* *aquifolium*; *Euonymus* (all varieties); *Senecio greyi*; *Buxus*; *Cineraria maritima*; *Hebe* (all varieties); *Cotinus coggygria*; *Cupressus macrocarpa* 'Donard Gold'; *Ruta graveolens* (rue); *Ilex* (holly); *Santolina chamaecyparissus*; *Weigela florida*; *Euphorbia wulfenii* and *Euphorbia epithymoides*; *Viburnum tinus*.

Large leaves: *Arum italicum* 'Pictum'; *Bergenia*; *Hosta fortunei* 'Albopicta', also *Hosta* 'Aurea' and *Hosta* 'Aureomarginata'; *Alchemilla mollis* (lady's mantle); *Heuchera*; *Tellima grandiflora*; *Hedera colchica* 'Variegata'; *Pelargonium*; *Fatsia japonica*.

Trailing foliage: *Hedera* (ivy), many varieties including *H. helix* 'Goldheart' and 'Glacier'; *Vinca major* 'Variegata'; *Ballota pseudodictamnus*; *Lonicera japonica*; *Cotoneaster salicifolius*.

It isn't as necessary for the flower arranger to grow her own flowers, as there is usually a good selection of flowers available from florists all year round. So if you have a small garden, give priority to good foliage plants.

But garden flowers have a delicacy and a charm that escapes bought flowers. The essential flower in any flower arranger's garden, to my mind, is the rose. Roses blend happily with most other flowers, and a solitary rose, with its own foliage, in a slender container is a perfect arrangement in itself. The old shrub roses with their delightful scents are even more useful for providing graceful branches of loose blooms than the tidier and more sculptured modern roses.

There are two roses I would not like to be without. The first is *Rosa* 'Glenfiddich'—an amber-coloured floribunda (now known as cluster-flowered). This rose has superb foliage which can be preserved with glycerine (see page 58), it blooms almost continuously throughout the summer and is relatively resistant to disease.

My other favourite is the climber *R.* 'Compassion'. This is a tidy climber suitable for any house wall, only reaching 3 m (10 ft) in height, and it is also repeat flowering. Its colour is a beautiful mix of soft pink suffused with pale gold at the base. Mine took a year to produce good flowers but, once established in a warm corner, it is seldom without flowers in the summer.

Sweet peas (*Lathyrus odoratus*), like roses, must be garden-grown to achieve their full delicacy and range of superb colours. A mixture of sweet peas, roses and carnations is one of the most charming and heady combinations there is.

Most annuals, particularly cottage-types such as *Nigella* (love-in-a-mist), cosmos and delphinium, have an indefinable appeal and bring a particular charm to a flower arrangement. If you have room these three plus nicotiana, molucella and the perennial *Aquilegia* (Granny bonnets), rudbeckia and scabious are all well worth growing.

Though by no means a comprehensive list of plants for flower arranging, these will give you a varied selection from which to choose.

YOUR FIRST ARRANGEMENTS

9
A Vertical or Upright Design

If the theory of flower arrangement on the preceding pages doesn't mean a lot to you at the moment, it will. Come back to those chapters after you have had more practice in putting flowers together and creating your own designs. Words like form, proportion, balance, scale, contrast, harmony and so on will then be very relevant.

A vertical flower arrangement has a strong upward movement or line—almost severe, but it is a useful design for displaying a few flowers to perfection. It is also a good arrangement for a beginner, because it is probably very different from anything you have done before and will make you feel quite excited about your achievement. You will learn to appreciate the different shapes and textures of foliage and how to create a flowing line of flowers through a design, which is basic to all flower arranging.

31

The first placement of the three vertical strap leaves is something you will repeat in many other arrangements, where a strong vertical outline is needed, as in a pedestal, for instance. The use of bold, round leaves at the base and centre of an arrangement is frequently used to 'solidify' a design and give it a satisfying depth. The third foliage is used as a 'filler' and is chosen as an intermediate leaf size and shape, between the two.

You will need:

Foliage – Three long strap-shaped leaves, such as iris, crocosmia, phormium or yucca. Three large flat leaves, such as bergenia or hosta. Six or seven short sprays of a smaller-leaved, branching foliage with a different shape and texture, such as *Escallonia* 'Apple blossom'; *Senecio greyi*; rosemary; cotoneaster.

Flowers – Seven irises.

Mechanics – Oasis fix; a plastic frog; a flat dish about 25 cm (10 in) in diameter; a small block of oasis about 7 cm (3 in) square and 5 cm (2 in) deep.

Use a small piece of oasis fix to fasten the frog about two-thirds of the way across the dish from the front. Soak the oasis and press it down on the frog.

Cut the first strap leaf to a finished length of at least one-and-a-half times the width of the dish, allowing for the stem end inserted in the oasis. Position the leaf towards the back of the oasis, leaning very slightly backwards. It should be turned very slightly to one side. Cut the next leaf about 6 cm (2½ in) shorter, place this in front of the first, leaning slightly left. Cut the third leaf about 4 cm (1½ in) shorter than the previous one and position to the right, in front, facing sideways. Be careful not to line them up. Place them as though they are growing from the same central point, inside the oasis.

Shorten the stems of the flat leaves so that only a small amount of stem will be above the oasis and insert these, one behind the tallest strap leaf at two o'clock and the others to the front at about five o'clock and eight o'clock. Cut a stem of the escallonia about 5 cm (2 in) shorter than the shortest strap leaf and place between the three upright leaves. Add a second

Strap leaves such as iris or phormium

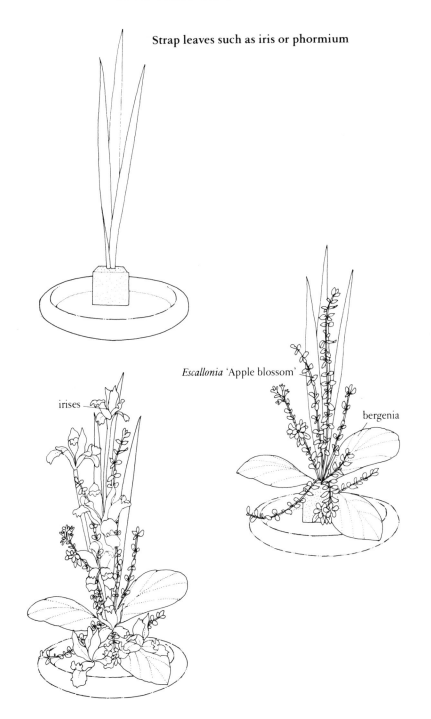

Escallonia 'Apple blossom'

irises

bergenia

slightly shorter branch to the back, and several much shorter branches, graded in height, to fill in at the front. All the branches should appear to 'grow' from the same point as the other foliage.

Stand back and look at this arrangement of foliage. If you are not happy with it, rearrange it until you are. With practice, you will be able to achieve a balanced look instinctively. Until then, you may be aware of something not being quite right: the proportions or the height are wrong, for example, and it is just a case of working at it until the outline pleases you. The oasis should be hidden by the round leaves, but you can also add a few pebbles or small stones to make sure it can't be seen.

When you are happy with the framework of foliage, add the irises. Cut the flowers to grade them in height. The least open flower should be the tallest and placed to the top and back of the arrangement. The largest flower should have the shortest stem and be at the base, with the others between them. Again, don't line them up, but try to achieve movement in the way they are placed with the foliage in a gently curving line.

10
An Asymmetrical Design

Now let's take arranging flowers a step further. You have made a vertical design. If we now follow the same upright line but add a leg to make an L-shaped design and fill it out a bit, we will have an asymmetrical triangle.

Flower arrangements are given geometric names to identify the basic shape of the design, but you are not going to end up with a rigid triangle, either symmetrical or asymmetrical. You are aiming now at enlarging on the vertical design and producing a flowing, lopsided design, loosely based on an asymmetrical triangle. See the colour section.

You will define the shape with the tips of the foliage and keep within that shape, but your flowers and foliage should look unrestrained and appear to flow naturally from one central point.

An asymmetrical design looks as though it is difficult to achieve, but it is quite simple. It is easiest to execute on a flat base with no visible container and therefore it is a good choice for a hall table, alcove, wide shelf or windowsill at home, or for a church window or vestibule.

This arrangement starts with a base. Bases are collected by flower arrangers and you will have to start a collection of them yourself. A base is used to add visual weight to an arrangement, or as the starting point of a design or simply to protect a polished surface. Bases can be made of wood, bark, slate, cork, fabric-covered board such as a cake board, or cut and painted plywood. Any shape can be cut, or bases can be purchased from flower shops in round, oval and kidney shapes.

For the starting point of this design, buy or cut a kidney-shaped base 25 × 50 cm (10 × 20 in) at the widest parts. Cover the board with a textured green fabric, such as cotton velvet. If you can track down a greyish-green colour (and the colour of oasis is perfect), you will find this a really useful base for many different arrangements.

To cover the base, lay the fabric wrong-side up on a table. Place the base on top and cut round the outline, allowing an extra 3 cm (1¼ in) all round. Spread clear-drying glue on the vertical edge of the board. Press the fabric against the edge and leave to dry. Snip the fabric at intervals of about 1 cm (½ in) almost, but not quite, to the stuck edge. Spread glue on the board underneath the turning of fabric and press the fabric down on to the board. Ease up the fabric and trim to lie flat.

With a round base you can simply hem the fabric and thread a length of elastic through it. The fabric is then removable. With the kidney shape, it isn't possible to get a really smooth result that way. The edges of bases can be defined with a matching braid or narrow velvet ribbon.

You should be able to track down the foliage for this design easily. I have suggested some of the commonest garden foliages and florist's flowers that are available all year round. If you have to substitute, keep to the same form and leaf shape.

You will need:

Foliage – *Berberis darwinii*; *Ribes sanguineum* (flowering currant); *Hedera canariensis* 'Variegata' (variegated ivy); narrow strap leaves such as crocosmia or *Chlorophytum* (spider plant).

Flowers – Seven large-flowered carnations; 3 or 4 sprays of lilies; freesias in colours to link the colour of the lilies and carnations; spray carnations in a deeper shade of the colour of the large carnations.

Mechanics – Oasis and holder, or a shallow tin or dish (if necessary, paint the tin green so that it will not be visible through the leaves); florist's tape; a kidney-shaped base.

Wedge the soaked oasis in the container, leaving 5–8 cm (2–3 in) above the rim, and tape it securely. Place both the oasis and container on the base, off centre to the left and back of the board.

Although the first three stems of berberis are used to give the upright line as in the previous vertical arrangement, choose slightly curving branches for a gentler line. Cut the first branch to approximately one-and-a-half times the width of the base. Place it towards the back of the oasis and leaning very slightly

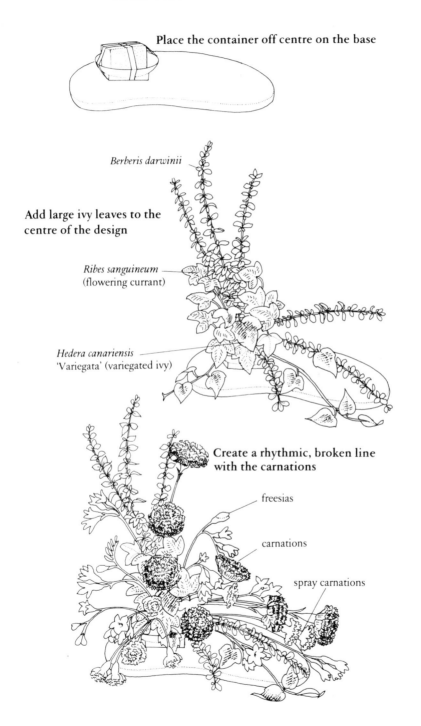

Place the container off centre on the base

Berberis darwinii

Add large ivy leaves to the centre of the design

Ribes sanguineum (flowering currant)

Hedera canariensis 'Variegata' (variegated ivy)

Create a rhythmic, broken line with the carnations

freesias

carnations

spray carnations

backwards. Cut the second slightly shorter and place this behind and to the left of the first, but appearing to come from the same point in the oasis. Add the third upright stem to the front from the same point, but leaning slightly forward.

Cut a branch of berberis approximately two-thirds of the length of the tallest stem. Place this so that it appears to come from the same central point, curving forward at four o'clock. Place a slightly longer curving branch below this, at five o'clock. Place a much shorter one to come forward over the edge of the oasis. You now have the asymmetrical triangular outline, and no plant material should be added which will break this imaginary shape.

Add short sprays of ribes, to fill in the corner of the 'L'. Place one facing forwards and a longer one to the back behind the main branches. You will need two or three, depending on the quantity of foliage on each spray. Add a trail of ivy, flowing down over the edge of the base, amongst the two trails of berberis, a second trail to the left and two or three very large ivy leaves coming out from the centre.

Now add the flowers. Place the carnations, smallest to the top and the largest to the base, flowing down in a rhythmic, broken line. Place one slightly left of the main stem, but not too far, or you will end up with a triangle and not an asymmetrical triangle. Form the focal point with the largest flowers in the centre and place one to the extreme right to curve forward over the edge of the base.

Add the freesias following the shape of the foliage, making sure that they all appear to 'grow' from the central point. You will now have a satisfactory asymmetrical design, if somewhat static. Recess some of the small spray carnations throughout. (Remove the buds which are showing no colour. These continue to grow and look straggly, spoiling the outline as they rarely open out.) Allow longer sprays to curve to the sides at the base, to give vitality to the design. Add the lilies, graded in height, between the carnations. Be careful not to get the pollen from the lilies on your clothes. If you do, don't rub it in—use a piece of polyurethane foam to lift it off. Finally, insert several narrow strap leaves curving from the centre of the design over the flower heads.

11
A Symmetrical Design

The natural progression from the preceding flower arrangement is to make a symmetrical triangle design. This is now a
good stage to start experimenting with containers and to use
something you have not used for flowers before. Do you have a
bulbous, narrow-necked vase, an urn, a lamp base or a ginger
jar? It does not have to have a wide neck, or much of an opening
at all. You just have to devise a way of fixing the oasis securely
to the top. The container should have a fat solid shape to balance the visual weight of the mass of flowers. It will be slowly
dawning on you that as much advance planning can go into
fixing the oasis to a container as in choosing the flowers and
foliage! For an urn-shaped container, simply wedge a large
block of oasis into the neck so that about 10 cm (4 in) of the
oasis is above the opening.

For a container with a very narrow opening, wire or tape a
coffee jar lid, shallow tin or oasis holder to the top. If you are
using a plastic dish, bore small holes through it, at the top, and
insert wire through them. Line the dish with plastic to prevent
the water leaking.

It is also time to start being more adventurous in your choice
of foliage and to use a wider selection of leaf shapes and colours.

You will need:
Foliage – *Viburnum tinus*; stephanandra; *Hedera canariensis*
    'Variegata' (variegated ivy); *Vinca major* 'Elegantissima';
    fern; *Elaeagnus pungens* 'Maculata'; *Skimmia japonica*.
Flowers – Spray carnations; freesias; garden roses.
Mechanics – Urn or lamp base; wire, tape, oasis and holder.

Assemble the mechanics as described above. Make a strong
upward line with a branch of viburnum one-and-a-half times

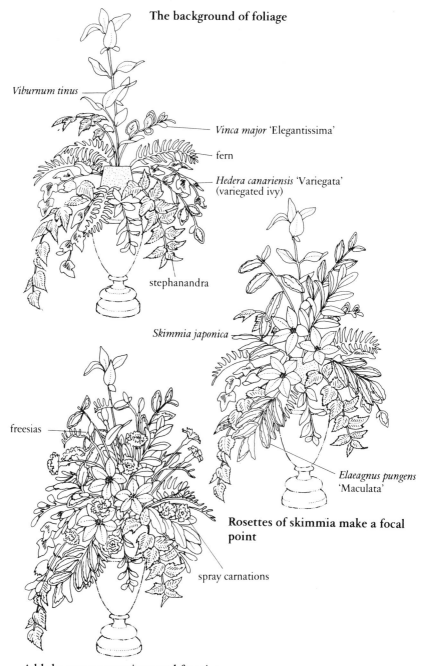

The background of foliage

Viburnum tinus

Vinca major 'Elegantissima'

fern

Hedera canariensis 'Variegata'
(variegated ivy)

stephanandra

Skimmia japonica

Elaeagnus pungens
'Maculata'

**Rosettes of skimmia make a focal
point**

freesias

spray carnations

Add the spray carnations and freesias

40

the height of the container. Outline the triangular shape with curving sprays of stephanandra, giving a downward sweep at each side. These branches should not be identical in length or you will get a very rigid, uniform triangle. Outline a loosely flowing background of foliage with shorter sprays of stephanandra, ivy, vinca and fern.

Fill in to the front and back with the more dense foliage of the elaeagnus and skimmia, placing three rosettes of skimmia to make a focal point.

Add the spray carnations, following the outline and bringing some forward over the lip of the container. Arrange the freesias in the same way, shortening the stems to recess some of them throughout the arrangement.

Add the roses, allowing some to curve gracefully to the front and sides, with the largest ones in the centre. (See the illustration on the front cover of the book.)

12
A Crescent Design

While creating the arrangements already described you should have learned to choose and place curving foliage in a graceful line, flowing from one central point. This is the basis of all natural looking flower arrangement.

Some types of foliage have stems you can bend to take the shape you need in an arrangement. Common broom (*Cytisus*) can be soaked and then tied into circles, allowed to dry and then untied and teased into sweeping curves, which are excellent for outlining a design. The other foliage in this design is *Senecio greyi*, which forms graceful curves at the ends of the branches, particularly on unpruned shrubs.

This crescent-shaped design is quick to do and will not only give you confidence in shaping foliage, it is also a very effective way of making the most of the first summer rose or a few prize peonies. It is useful too for displaying an accessory, such as a photograph or a special plate. The crescent design doesn't need a lot of foliage either, but to be effective it must have the foliage appearing to grow as a complete curve. This is very good practice for you in assembling the focal point of any arrangement effectively and in taking flowers in a flowing line through a design.

You will need:
Foliage – *Cytisus praecox* (broom); *Senecio greyi*; 3 large hosta leaves.
Flowers – Garden roses.
Mechanics – Round or oval base; plate or photograph; plate stand; oasis and holder; florist's tape.

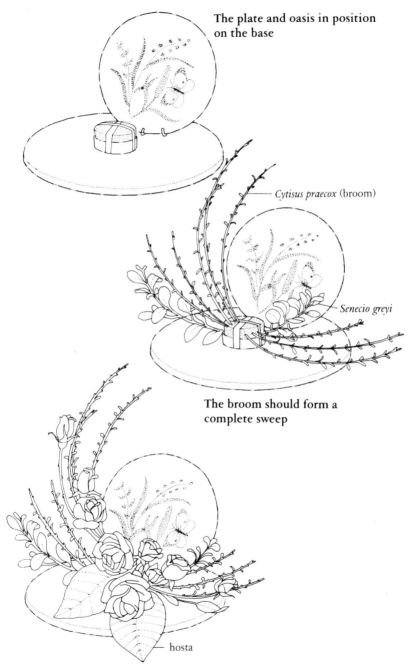

The plate and oasis in position on the base

Cytisus praecox (broom)

Senecio greyi

The broom should form a complete sweep

hosta

The heads of the roses follow the curve

Position the plate or photograph on a small stand to the back and right of the base. You may need to raise it about 5 cm (2 in), depending on the size. Place the oasis holder with the oasis taped securely in place at the base of the plate to the left. Place two curved branches of broom, one in each side of the oasis, so that they appear as one complete sweep.

Add slightly shorter sprays of senecio following the curve. Place the hosta leaves towards the centre to hide the oasis.

Place the roses to follow the outline. Start with the smallest buds on curving stems, placing these to follow the outer arms of the curve. Add larger, more open blooms, working towards the centre and base of the design. Place the full blown roses in the centre and coming forward in the arrangement, facing the front. The heads of the other roses should be turned to follow the direction of the curve.

13
An Inverted Crescent Design

A further development of the curving line is my favourite design—an inverted crescent. This is done in a raised container or on a pedestal, which gives a feeling of lightness, enhanced by curving sprays and trails of foliage. It is a useful shape for an alcove or a table centre, and if you add candles, it is perfect for a buffet or dinner table.

Let's do this one on a tall candlestick, so that you will learn about adapting a candlestick for flowers. Buy a plastic candle cup from a florist and spray or paint it green or to match the candlestick. Candle cups come in several sizes, so choose one large enough to hold the oasis and a good fit for the candlestick. Secure the cup in the candlestick with oasis fix, tape or wire. If you are using the candlestick only for flower arrangement, bore small holes in the sides of the cup and wire it in place permanently.

You will need:

Foliage – *Cytisus* (broom); *Lonicera* (honeysuckle); *Vinca major* 'Elegantissima'; *Hedera canariensis* 'Variegata' (variegated ivy).

Flowers – Spray carnations; *Viburnum farreri*; mixed freesias; garden roses.

Mechanics – Candlestick and candle cup; oasis and fix; tape; two florist's candle holders; two tall candles.

Secure the candle cup as described above and tape the oasis in place. Shorten one candle by cutting 2.5 cm (1 in) off the base. Press a small piece of oasis fix to the base of each candle and push the candles into the holders. This keeps them firmly upright. Insert the candle holders in the centre of the oasis.

Bend the broom into graceful sweeps and place one to each side of the candles and four shorter pieces to the centre, sides

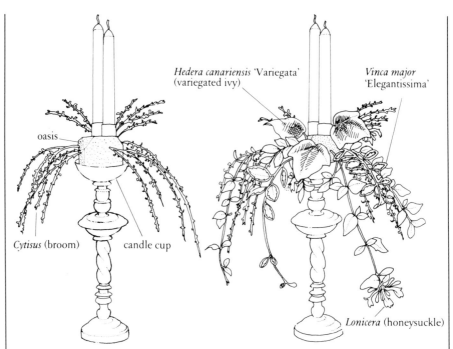

Hedera canariensis 'Variegata' (variegated ivy)

Vinca major 'Elegantissima'

oasis

Cytisus (broom)

candle cup

Lonicera (honeysuckle)

The side sweeps of broom should be of unequal length

Large ivy leaves form the focal point of the foliage

and back. The side sweeps should not be exactly the same length or the arrangement will look too uniform.

Add longer, gracefully curving sprays of honeysuckle to each side and one to the front and slightly left of centre. Add trails of vinca to the left side, top and back. Place three large ivy leaves to form the focal point of the foliage.

Position the taller spray carnations to follow the side curves, and place shorter curving sprays to the back and front of the design. Remove the foliage from the branches of viburnum. Place to the centre in front of the candlesticks, where the flower-heads will soften the base of the candles.

Add longer sprays of viburnum trailing to each side and to the front and back, within the outline formed by the carnations. Fill in any gaps in the outline with freesias. Finally add the roses, the buds and the longest stems to the outer sides and the open blooms to the centre. (See illustration in the colour section.)

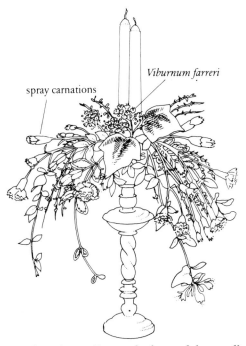

spray carnations

Viburnum farreri

Soften the outline at the base of the candles

14
The Hogarth Curve

Some years ago a grand and sweeping Hogarth curve was the mark of a good flower arranger. The design was named after the English painter, William Hogarth, whose paintings are evidence of his love of asymmetrical curves. It is also called the lazy-S design. Because the current fashion in flower arranging is for looser, softer effects, this line arrangement is no longer as popular as it once was. However, it is a very stylish, impressive design, and was thought to be difficult. Now, with the advent of oasis, it isn't. But it looks impressive! Also if you really want to master flower arranging and execute loose flowing designs with ease, then try the Hogarth curve, because you will learn more about balance and line, focal points and rhythm from this design than from any other. Many of the most attractive arrangements of flowers in a jug or teapot are simply modifications of the Hogarth curve.

You will need:
Foliage – *Cytisus* (broom); *Senecio greyi*; *Ligustrum ovalifolium* 'Aureo-marginatum' (golden privet); hosta.
Flowers – *Rosa* 'Glenfiddich'; *Lilium* 'First Love'.
Mechanics – Oasis; a tall slender container, candlestick or narrow-necked jug; a small piece of chicken wire.

Wedge the oasis into the neck of the container. Because of the narrowness of the container, only a small piece of oasis can be used, so place chicken wire over the oasis and twist or tape the edges securely to the container. This gives additional support to the longest curving branches.

If you use a candlestick or a container with a very narrow neck, use a candle cup as in the previous arrangement.

Bend two lengths of cytisus and insert into the oasis so that they outline a complete sweeping curve. Cut two sprays of

Use chicken wire for additional support

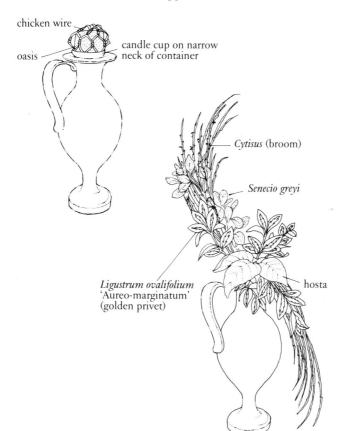

chicken wire

oasis

candle cup on narrow
neck of container

Cytisus (broom)

Senecio greyi

Ligustrum ovalifolium
'Aureo-marginatum'
(golden privet)

hosta

Hosta leaves placed at the focal point

senecio slightly shorter than the cytisus and following the same curve. Trim away superfluous leaves to give a bold line. Add these to follow the outline. Add a shorter, fuller spray to the centre. Place two sprays of golden privet at the centre of the curve and three large hosta leaves at the focal point.

Add the roses to follow the outline, with the smallest to the tips of the curves and the largest and most open to the centre. Finally, add the lilies at the heart of the arrangement. Do not cut the stems too short, as the lilies need to come forward in the design to avoid looking flat. (See the colour section.)

15
A Pedestal Arrangement

You can now think big and combine all you have learned so far to execute a large pedestal arrangement for a church, wedding or simply in a hall or room large enough not to be overpowered by it.

The most usual outline for a pedestal arrangement is the symmetrical triangle, but if you are doing a pair of pedestals in a church, for example, it is often more pleasing to create two asymmetrical triangles complementing each other. If your church doesn't have a pedestal, you will have to invest in one. Large florists, garden centres and church suppliers stock them. The wrought iron types are excellent; they give a lightness to an arrangement and can be used for displaying plants when not in use for flowers.

Big arrangements not only need greater quantities and variety of plant material, they also need larger leaves and flowers. If a pedestal is filled up with small flowers and sprays of fussy foliage, it looks very unrestful and cluttered.

The mechanics for a large pedestal arrangement need some care, as the great weight of plant material will topple over if not secured. Some pedestals come with their own containers, but if not, use a heavy flat-based bowl such as a dog's large bowl or a bulb bowl.

You will need:

Foliage – *Eucalyptus gunnii*; bay laurel; *Rubus tricolor*; *Fatsia japonica*; *Weigela florida* 'Variegata'; *Phormium cookianum*; *Jasminum nudiflorum*.

Flowers – Carnations; garden roses; alstroemeria; *Lilium* 'Stargazer'.

Mechanics – Bowl; pedestal; two plastic frogs; oasis fix; oasis; florist's tape.

The outline foliage

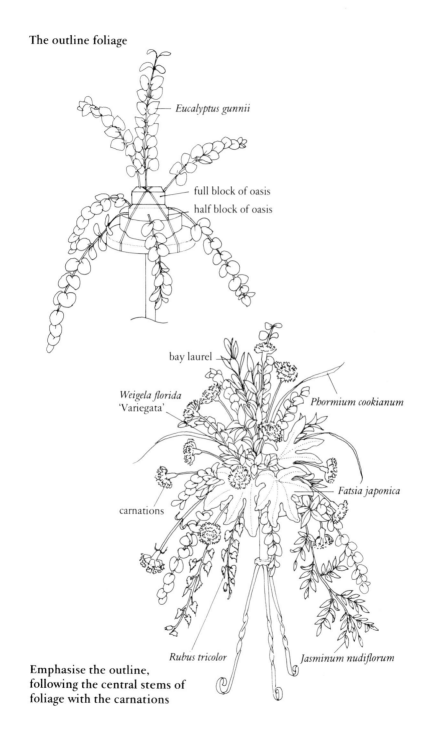

Eucalyptus gunnii

full block of oasis
half block of oasis

bay laurel

Weigela florida 'Variegata'

Phormium cookianum

carnations

Fatsia japonica

Rubus tricolor

Jasminum nudiflorum

Emphasise the outline, following the central stems of foliage with the carnations

Position the bowl centrally on the pedestal. Fasten the plastic frogs in the dry bowl with oasis fix. Wedge one large block of oasis end on to the back of the bowl, and place a second block, cut to fit the bowl, flat end to the front. Tape the oasis-filled bowl securely to the pedestal and make sure it is stable.

As with all flower arrangements, the outline of the design is set up first with the 'line' foliage. The height of the first, central placement depends on the type of pedestal and the foliage. A delicate wrought iron pedestal, for example, will take very tall, finely arched sprays, but look top heavy with the same length of branches of evergreen. A marble pillar, on the other hand, will need both height and visual weight to look balanced.

Use the first three sprays of eucalyptus to define the triangular shape and the height and width of the arrangement. Position a straight central branch two-thirds of the way from the front of the oasis. Place two curving branches to define the outer points of the triangle. These side placements should not be exactly even in length and should follow a graceful downwards line. The rest of the plant material should be within the outline formed by this triangle. Place shorter branches to the sides of the main stem, and a spray coming forward to the front. Make sure that the outline foliage is a satisfying shape and that the height and width are balanced in relation to the pedestal.

Fill in with foliage. Add sprays of bay laurel between the eucalyptus and to the front and back. Place long sprays of rubus curving forwards to the left. Remember to keep adding shorter sprays of foliage behind the main stem as you work, or the arrangement will become weighted to the front and may lean— or worse, fall—forwards. Also, because a pedestal arrangement is usually viewed from a distance, step back from time to time to see how your work is progressing.

Place three or four very large fatsia leaves at the heart and weigela interspersed through the design. Add arching spears of phormium to follow and strengthen the outline.

Use carnations to follow the central stems of the foliage, and to curve downwards to the sides and front. Add gently curving sprays of jasmine to the right side to balance the rubus on the left. Fill in with the garden roses and alstroemeria and, finally, add the lilies to the central focal point. (See the colour section.)

16
Using Driftwood

Driftwood is not just those pieces of wood which have drifted in with the tide and have weathered to a silvery grey. The term driftwood includes any wood used as part of a flower arrangement—from pieces of bark and contorted twigs to tree trunks, heavy branches and roots. The gnarled and twisted shape of leafless branches, the rough texture and attractive markings in the grain of a wood and the subtleties of colour in different types of wood all add a new dimension to the art of arranging flowers.

Because it is a natural element, wood blends in beautifully with most other plant material and it isn't difficult to use driftwood in a flower arrangement. It looks 'arty', and that can be due more to the properties of the wood than the skill of the flower arranger. It can also add interest and a rustic element to a design.

Looking for driftwood is a pleasant reason for a country walk. Take home any wood with an interesting shape but remember not to raid private woodland! Even if you cannot think of a use for it immediately, you will! Look for branches with interesting shapes on river banks, sea shores and wasteland. Exposed roots on fallen trees often have amazingly contorted shapes. Tree ivy is another good source of twisted shapes. Soak the thick ivy stems for twenty-four hours and the bark will peel off to reveal a smooth white wood underneath.

Use smaller twisted branches as an outline or to give height to an arrangement. Thicker pieces of wood make excellent containers for flowers. Bore a hole in the wood large enough to hold a water bowl. A tall heavy branch can be fixed firmly to a base and containers wired to the stem, to allow several small flower arrangements to trail up the stem.

Driftwood must be treated before use. First make sure the wood is hard and not rotten. It may have rotten bits attached to it, but the main core should be sound. Scrape away any soft wood, mud and debris with a pointed knife and a wire brush. As you work on the wood, the shape changes and the markings are revealed. Incidentally, it can take hours of gentle scraping to get down to the hard wood grain beneath the debris.

Next scrub the wood with mild household bleach to kill any lurking insects. Grey, weathered wood, however, should only be washed gently in mild soapy water so that the greyish tones are not lost. Tree roots usually need only a good scrub to remove the dirt. Trim when dry to a pleasing shape.

The driftwood can then be left in this natural state and just rubbed hard to give it a sheen, or you can apply several coats of wax polish or linseed oil, which darkens the wood. To give a greyish tinge, soak the wood for several days in a solution of 225 g (½ lb) salt dissolved in 4.5 litres (1 gal) water. Leave in the sun to dry. Soaking overnight in a solution of household bleach (1 litre (1½ pt) bleach to 4.5 litres (1 gal) water) gives a yellowish tone to most woods. A light stain may improve the colour, but don't be tempted to varnish it, as it will look too artificial to blend with plant material.

After treating the wood, try placing it several different ways to find the best line. Then you have to devise a way of making it stand at that angle. Add a 'leg' of a small piece of dowelling or several pieces of wood to hold it in position, or use a loop of heavy wire with the ends pushed into the wood, where it will not be seen. Driftwood clamps, incorporating a pin holder, are sometimes available to hold large pieces of wood securely. If you can't find one, a carpenter's small clamp can be adapted.

A large screw can be screwed through the underside of a wooden base, with the point upwards and the end of the driftwood screwed down onto this. Driftwood can also be made to stand by mixing Polyfilla into a thick paste, forming it into a mound and pressing the end of the wood in this, supporting it until it sets hard. The base will be covered by stones, foliage or moss in an arrangement.

Several pieces of wood with interesting shapes can be joined together with a couple of concealed screws. Very often, some of the large pieces of contorted driftwood used in large flower displays have been assembled from several small pieces by someone with a good eye for an original line.

Small lightweight pieces of wood will stand in a pin holder and are ideal for a simple but effective display of daffodils as their stems and leaves are not easily pushed into oasis.

DRIFTWOOD WITH DAFFODILS

You will need:
Foliage – Elaeagnus pungens 'Maculata'; Helleborus foetidus.
Flowers – Daffodils.
Mechanics – Pin holder; small, shallow dish to hold the pin holder and water; oasis fix; a wooden or hessian-covered base; a small piece of driftwood.

Secure the pin holder to the base of the dish with oasis fix. Place the dish to the back and left of the covered base. Press the driftwood onto the pins of the holder, two-thirds of the way to the back.

To create a natural look, place the flowers first, in a group, with several of their own leaves, varying the heights and facing in different directions, just as they grow. Place the shorter flowers to the front of the group, but arrange them all vertically, in a natural way. Daffodils last better in a pin holder in water rather than in oasis, which blocks their hollow stems.

Add short sprays of elaeagnus to the back and each side of the group and place three large hellebore leaves, one to the back and the others to cover the pin holder. (See overleaf.)

DRIFTWOOD PLANT HOLDER

A large piece of driftwood or a sturdy branch can be wedged firmly into a base made from a thick section cut from a tree trunk. Several containers are then fixed at different heights and the plant material arranged in them to flow down the length of the branch. This is an original way of displaying flowers, particularly in a confined space or corner, or in a church. A plant holder like this is rewarding to make, as you will find a number of uses for it.

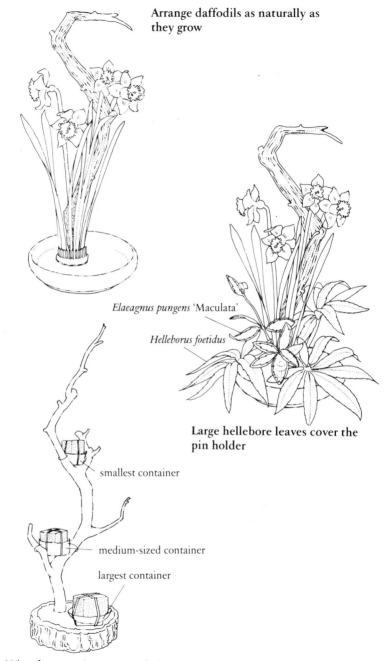

Arrange daffodils as naturally as
they grow

Elaeagnus pungens 'Maculata'

Helleborus foetidus

Large hellebore leaves cover the
pin holder

smallest container

medium-sized container

largest container

Wire the containers securely in position

Choose a sturdy branch with several definite curves and side branches. Look at the piece of wood carefully and decide on two main side branches, one near the top and the other about half way down the length. Trim away surplus branches, but leave a few side shoots to give a natural outline.

To make the base, drill a hole into a thick, heavy cross-cut of a tree trunk, slightly off centre. Make the hole slightly less than the diameter of the branch and file down the end of the branch to wedge it very firmly into the base.

You will need three containers, graded in size. Plastic dishes or deep-sided lids are suitable. Drill two holes on opposite sides of the two smallest containers, near the top. Thread thin wire through these holes and wire the containers securely to the wood, so that they nestle in a fork of the branch. The third container sits on the base at the foot of the branch.

ALL-FOLIAGE ARRANGEMENT

Natural wood looks good with any type of flowers, or even none at all. Try using a branch for an all-foliage design. This will be a good exercise in making you more aware of the diversity of colour, shape and texture in different foliages.

You will need:
Foliage – *Cotoneaster franchetii*; *Fagus* (beech); *Hedera colchica* 'Variegata' (variegated ivy); heuchera; hosta; *Choisya ternata* 'Sundance'.
Mechanics – Oasis; driftwood triple holder; florist's tape.

Cut the oasis to fit the three containers and secure with tape. Choose curving sprays of cotoneaster and arrange some in each container to flow down, following the outline of the main branch and trailing over the front of the base. Add short sprays of beech to echo the outline, and trails of ivy to lighten the design. Place single leaves of heuchera to the outside of each container and hosta leaves towards the centre. Insert rosettes of choisya at the heart of each arrangement to resemble flowers and create a centre of interest. (See the colour section.)

PRESERVING FLOWERS AND FOLIAGE

17
Preserving with Glycerine

It is well known that beech leaves can be preserved with glycerine, and a jug of russet coloured sprays of beech is a popular decoration during the winter months. What is not so well known is that many other useful foliages will preserve as well as and often better than beech and there are several ways in which they can be used in flower arrangement.

Mature, though not old, plant material can be preserved at any time during the summer—the end of July to the beginning of August being the best time—while the sap is still rising. Pick foliage in good condition, unblemished, on a dry day. Beech branches up to 1.5 m (5 ft) in length will take up glycerine, so don't cut all the sprays of plant material short or to the same length. My own favourite foliage to treat with glycerine is rose leaves. If you choose healthy bronze-green foliage, such as that of *Rosa* 'Glenfiddich', it will keep most of its colour rather than turning brown or cream like some glycerined foliage. During winter the rose foliage can be used in fresh flower arrangements or dried flower displays.

Glycerine is available from chemists. Plants absorb the glycerine in dilute form through the stem and leaves to replace the natural moisture. With a few exceptions, such as delphiniums and larkspur, the annual amaranthus, *Alchemilla mollis* (lady's mantle) and gypsophila, flowers don't absorb glycerine readily, so the glycerine method is best for foliage and some seedheads.

To make up a glycerine solution, mix one measure of glycerine to two measures of boiling water and mix thoroughly. Use at once; although plants continue to absorb the mixture when cold, they take much longer to preserve if started in a cold solution. Pour the solution into several tall glass jars. Coffee jars are ideal as in them it is easy to check the level of the liquid as it is absorbed. Place the newly cut stems in the hot glycerine solution to a depth of 5–7 cm (2–3 in). Do not overcrowd the jars as the leaves may be crushed out of shape. Stand the jars in a cool room, out of direct sunlight.

The surface of large single leaves, such as fatsia, standing in glycerine should be wiped occasionally with a glycerine-soaked sponge to help it absorb the solution. Any leaves with a tough, smooth surface, such as camellia and *Aucuba japonica* (spotted laurel), may be preserved by being floated in a dish of glycerine solution.

The length of time taken to absorb the glycerine varies with each plant, from one to eight weeks. Check the foliage daily. When it is pliable, slightly oily and has changed colour, remove it from the solution. Over-preserved material sweats glycerine and is prone to mildew. Any left-over solution can be re-heated and re-used.

Glycerine always changes the colour of plant material. The final colour is influenced by the time of year the foliage is picked, the amount of light the leaves get during the preserving process and the length of time they are in the solution. Most foliage turns varying shades of brown. Beech, for example, turns a very dark green if glycerined in midsummer and a copper bronze in the early autumn. Ruscus and choisya always turn cream. Any glycerined foliage will be lightened by standing it on a sunny windowsill when the glycerine process is complete.

It is worth trying any foliage with the glycerine treatment, but these are the ones that I have found to be the most successful. The approximate time each takes is given in brackets: *Pyrus* (1 week); beech, eucalyptus (10 days); rose, pittosporum (2 weeks); ferns (2–3 weeks); mahonia, *Buxus* (box), cotoneaster (3 weeks); *Choisya ternata*, camellia, *Laurus* (laurel) (4 weeks); Cupressus, *Fatsia japonica* (5 weeks); aspidistra (8 weeks).

Glycerined material is quite tough and will last for years if carefully stored when not in use. It is best stored flat, in shallow boxes between sheets of tissue paper to protect it from dust. If it gets crushed, you can revive it by holding it over steam. Ironing it with a steam iron is also most successful. Dusty leaves can be wiped with a damp cloth and dried.

18
Air-drying

All flowers can be preserved by air-drying, although a few, mentioned before, can be glycerined or air-dried. Many plants dry naturally in the garden, but this process can be improved upon by bringing the plants inside and giving them ideal conditions in which to dry evenly and avoid the ravages of the weather.

Some of the most successful and decorative dried flowers are: *Acanthus mollis*; *Achillea* (yarrow); *Alchemilla mollis* (lady's mantle); *Amaranthus caudatus* (love-lies-bleeding); delphinium and larkspur in colours of blue, pink, white and lavender; *Centaurea cyanus* (cornflower); *Echinops* (globe thistle); gypsophila; liatris; rosebuds; *Salvia horminum* (clary); *Solidago* (golden rod). Florist's small rosebuds or tight buds of garden roses can be air-dried or preserved with a desiccant (see page 63).

Foliage can be dried but is usually not as successful as glycerined foliage. *Senecio greyi* is an exception. The foliage keeps its greyish tinge better if air-dried. Many grasses and seedheads dry well and are useful to add interest to a dried arrangement.

Cut flowers for drying after a spell of good weather and just before they are fully open. Pick seedheads just as they are beginning to dry naturally. Thistles, bulrushes and pampas grass should be picked when they are only half open, as they continue to open indoors. Remove the leaves and tie the stems in small bunches. Suspend them upside-down in a dry, warm, preferably dark place with plenty of air: an airing cupboard is ideal.

Hydrangea is an exception. Pick it when the bracts are papery and allow it to dry out slowly, with the stem ends standing in a little water. Make sure the water does not evaporate completely before the heads have dried out, which could take several weeks.

Certain small flowers, particularly gypsophila, statice and tight bud roses, can be partially dried in a microwave oven before being air-dried, which saves time. Other flowers may also work well, so experiment with a few to see what happens.

To dry flowers in the microwave, strip off all the foliage and place the flowers head to tail on several layers of kitchen paper. Do not cover. Use a medium setting (400–500W) for about two to three minutes. Check, and replace the kitchen paper if it is damp before repeating. The flowers should feel like slightly damp paper. Remove and hang upside-down to dry completely.

Flower petals for pot pourri (see page 75) can also be partially dried in the microwave.

Dried plant material is fragile and needs more care than glycerined material in storage. Keep it in florist's cardboard boxes, supporting large heads on crumpled tissue paper. In general, dried flowers do not last as long as glycerined material and may continue to fade even after careful drying.

19
Preserving with Desiccants

Desiccants absorb the moisture from flowers but enable them to keep their shape, unlike dried flowers. Using desiccants is a challenging method of preserving flowers, because the results vary from very life-like blooms with good colour and shape to a nasty faded collection of greyish specimens! Success depends on picking the flowers at the best stage and removing them from the desiccant at just the right moment.

Silica gel is the desiccant most often used, and although initially it is expensive, it can be dried in the oven and used repeatedly. It is available in sugar-like crystals from chemists. It is worthwhile investing in a fair quantity of silica gel if you are going to do a lot of preserving. You will also find it useful for the apple-head flower seller on page 86.

Washed sand, borax and alum are less effective desiccants. Sand is heavy and care is needed not to flatten the flower petals. It also takes quite a long time to completely dry the flowers. Borax and alum are light, but they can be difficult to work in between the petals and also take longer than silica gel. They are all less expensive than silica gel.

To dry flowers with silica gel, pick when completely dry, as any damp petals will go brown. Select open buds and flowers in the early stages of bloom. Fully open flowers will drop their petals once they are fully dried.

Cut the flowers, leaving a stem of about 4 cm (1½ in). As it is difficult to attach a false stem to fully dried and brittle flowers, it is helpful to hook a rose wire through the centre of the flower while the plant material is still fresh. Spread 4 cm (1½ in) of desiccant in the base of an airtight container. Large plastic ice cream containers are useful. Push the stems into the silica gel, upright and not touching. Carefully and evenly sprinkle the desiccant into and over the flower heads, making sure that desiccant fills the spaces between the petals. Every part of the flower must come into contact with the desiccant, and the shape it is at this stage will be the final shape. It cannot be changed when dried, so be careful not to weigh down the petals and crush or flatten them. Add the desiccant slowly, by degrees, around the flowers.

More flowers can be added in layers, but only dry one type of flower at a time, as the drying times vary. It is difficult to generalise about preserving times as each species of flower differs and the stage of development of individual flowers also has an effect. Small, delicate flowers take about a day; larger, open-faced flowers take about three days; buds and fleshier flowers take five to seven days. More than a week results in very brittle flowers.

It is a good idea to mark the position of one flower just below the surface and then keep checking this one to see how it is progressing. It should feel like dry paper. If it does not, leave it a little longer. When the drying time is complete carefully pour off the desiccant, letting it trickle through your fingers. Catch the flower heads gently in your hand. Heat the silica gel in a warm oven for an hour or until it is completely dry, leave until cold and re-use.

Longer stems can be added to the flowers by inserting them into dried hollow stems, or by wiring the rose wire, attached before preserving, to a false stem or stub wire, using fine wire. Cover the wire with florist's tape or stem wrap.

Tankard of roses (see page 13)

Asymmetrical design (see page 35)

Inverted crescent design (see page 45)

The Hogarth curve (see page 48)

Pedestal arrangement (see page 50)

All-foliage arrangement with driftwood (see page 57)

Arrangement of preserved material (see page 67)

Christmas flower arrangement (see page 81)

20
Everlasting Flowers

The true everlasting dried flower is the daisy-type helichrysum, or straw flower. Everlastings are very easy annuals to grow and are available in a wide range of colours. *Helichrysum bracteatum* is the most commonly grown variety. Modern varieties keep their colour better than they used to. *Lawrencellia rosea* (paper daisy) is a daintier flower than the usual straw flower. Other everlastings worth growing are *Helipterum (Rhodanthe) manglesii*, with dark-ringed centres and *Acroclinium roseum* (dainty pink or white daisies). *Limonium*, which includes popular sea lavender and statice, is now available in many more attractive shades than the harsh purple most often seen.

Xeranthemum annuum is a very dainty, easily grown annual everlasting in delicate shades of white, rose, pink and purple. Although the heads are small, they dry quickly and retain their stems which are wiry and often bend into attractive shapes. The small clusters of the tiny heads of *Ammobium alatum* (winged everlasting), which open at different times, should be picked when two-thirds of the group of flower heads are fully open.

Two good yellow everlastings are *Craspedia globosa* with its drumstick head and the orange yellow of *Gnaphalium* 'Fairy Gold' which has clusters of tiny double blooms. *Carlina acaulis* is a hardy perennial well worth searching for in the seed catalogues. It has huge heads up to 12 cm (5 in) across, either white or dull red in colour.

A mixture of everlastings will give a better arrangement than the regular, rounded forms of helichrysum used by itself, which is often seen arranged on its own into unattractive humps in baskets. Helichrysums shed their stems during drying, so pick the heads only and before they are fully open, as they continue to open in the warmth. Avoid very open blooms, which become concave when dry and are not attractive.

Straw flowers need false stems. These can be added after the heads have dried, but the false stem is more secure if it is added before the drying process. Buy 0.70 mm stub wires, which are ready cut into lengths from the florist. Push a wire through the centre of each flower. Turn over 5 mm (¼ in) at the end and pull back the wire until it embeds itself in the flower. The wire can be disguised later by binding it with florist's or stem tape. Push the wires into dry oasis to hold the flowers upright while they dry in a warm, dark place. Everlastings can be wired together into sprays to give more impact when combined with other flowers in an arrangement.

21
An Arrangement of Preserved Material

Flower arrangements using dried plant material can often be fussy and unsatisfying, partly because of the sameness of the texture of the dried flowers, but also because of the smallness of much of the material. To overcome both of these disadvantages, use bold sculptured shapes of foliage such as mahonia and aspidistra, and add a contrast in texture either in the choice of container or by adding an 'accessory', such as the copper kettle shown here.

You will need:
Foliage – *Molucella laevis*; *Mahonia* 'Charity'; bronze-dyed pampas grass; ruscus; *Fatsia japonica*; eucalyptus.
Flowers – *Achillea.*
Mechanics – Florist's tape; oasis (the dry foam especially for dried flower arrangements); footed container; large, covered, round base; copper kettle and stand.

Tape the oasis in the container and place it to the left of the base. Place the kettle on its stand to the right. Position a long curving spray of molucella to sweep round and over the kettle, and a second spray appearing to come from the same point within the oasis to the front, completing the arch around the kettle. Then add three other shorter sprays of molucella; one at the back behind the kettle; one to the left and one coming forward in the arrangement. Add six mahonia leaves between these sprays, following the direction of the curves.

Insert six sprays of pampas grass between the mahonia, and also coming forward. Fill in with the cream ruscus and add two fatsia leaves to the centre of the design. Add eucalyptus to emphasise the sweep of the molucella and trail over the front of the base and soften the outline.

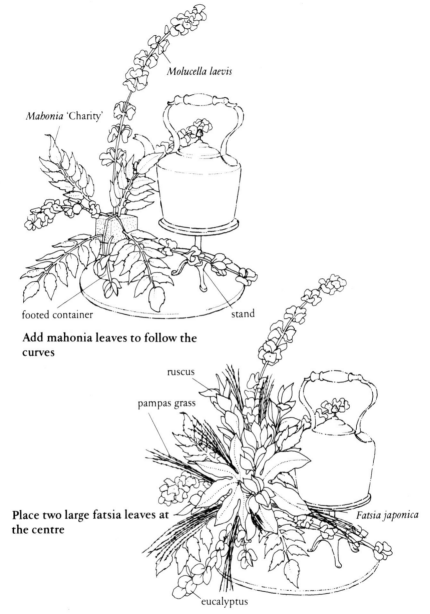

Molucella laevis

Mahonia 'Charity'

footed container   stand

Add mahonia leaves to follow the curves

ruscus

pampas grass

Place two large fatsia leaves at the centre

Fatsia japonica

eucalyptus

Finally, add the achillea to follow the outline round the kettle and to the front and sides. Recess some of the flowerheads to give depth, and leave others on longer stems to come forward at the centre of the arrangement. (See illustration in the colour section.)

22
A Wall-hanging of Preserved Foliage

Preserved foliage and flowers can also be combined in hanging garlands or ropes for draping over a mantelpiece or doorway, such as the Christmas garland on page 78, or made into a plaque on some kind of rigid backing to hang against a wall.

First decide on the hanging and devise a suitable backing. If the backing is there to hold the dry oasis and not part of the finished design, a strip of wood or very heavy card will do. If you want the backing larger than the arrangement of plant material and part of the design, a hessian-covered base or even a picture frame can be used. To make a longer plaque, the backing can be divided into sections and the units joined together. This way, although the finished effect is of one long plaque, the sections are graded in size allowing the plant material to taper gracefully at the end.

You will need:

Foliage – Rose leaves; *Mahonia* 'Charity'; box; fir cones; oak apples; golden cupressus; choisya.

Mechanics – Three cork tiles, each 20 cm (8 in) square; a curtain tie-back (1 m/39 in long) with tassel; wide adhesive tape; wire; dry oasis; glue.

Cut the corners off the first tile to form an oval about 20 cm (8 in) long and 18 cm (7 in) at the widest part. Cut the next tile 18 × 15 cm (7 × 6 in) and the last tile 15 × 10 cm (6 × 4 in). Knot the cord about 10 cm (4 in) from the top to form a loop. Place the tiles in a row one below the other, on the table, with the largest at the top and smallest at the bottom. Lay the doubled cord on top with the knot about 6 cm (2½ in) from the top tile and the tassel placed to hang below the bottom tile. Tape the cord to the back of the tiles, keeping the two cords apart, towards the sides of the ovals. On the right side, wire a

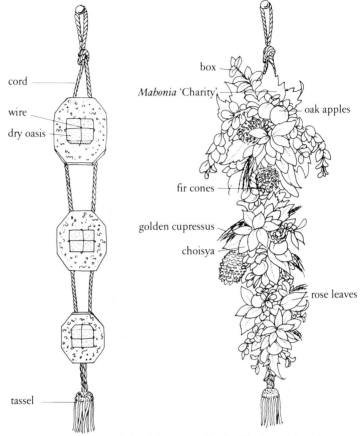

cord

wire

dry oasis

tassel

box

Mahonia 'Charity'

oak apples

fir cones

golden cupressus

choisya

rose leaves

Wire oasis to the cork backing   **The finished wall-hanging**

square of dry oasis to the centre of each oval, pushing the wires through the cork to the underside.

Cover the edges of the cork with rose leaves, pushing some into the oasis and gluing others to the cork at the outside edge.

Split the mahonia into single leaves and insert these into the outside of the oasis. Fill in to the side and front with box, leaving curving trails to the side, and overlap the spaces between each section.

Wire each fir cone with a stub wire twisted round the base and insert the wires into the oasis with the largest cones to the top of the design. Fill in with oak apples and small sprays of cupressus. Finally, add florets of choisya to form the centre of each unit.

23
Pressing Flowers

Another way to preserve plant material is by pressing. As with air-drying or drying with desiccants, pressing plants between absorbent paper removes the moisture, making the material last almost indefinitely. Pressed flowers retain their colour reasonably well, but as the flower-head is completely flat, its uses are restricted. Decorative uses for pressed flowers include pictures, cards, bookmarks, lampshades, book covers, door finger plates, paper weights and box lids. Pressed flower pictures are delightful to make, because they call on the skills of the flower arranger and require the continuing search for suitable material to press.

To retain their colour and press satisfactorily, flowers and leaves need to be left in a press for a minimum of eight weeks. Whether you make the picture for pleasure or profit or simply to give away, the most enjoyable way to organise this is to collect and press the material over a period of weeks during the summer and spend the dark winter evenings designing the pictures and gloating over the flowers and leaves when these are scarce.

When choosing plant material to press, look for flowers and leaves that are small in scale and pick them when they are in peak condition and absolutely dry. Pick only unblemished specimens.

However you intend to display the pressed flowers, good colour retention and perfectly unwrinkled specimens are needed, so although many flowers will press satisfactorily between the pages of an old telephone directory, it's worth buying a small press from a craft shop or making yourself a large 'pressing kit'.

You will need several 30–35 cm (12–14 in) squares of blockboard, and two squares of blotting paper of the same size for each board. Cover one board with the blotting paper. Spread out the flower-heads on the paper, using tweezers for

71

the smaller flowers. Do not allow the plants to touch. Carefully cover them with a second sheet of blotting paper and then with the second board. Put a heavy weight such as two bricks on top. Layers of flowers can be built up with a flat board between each layer enclosed between two sheets of blotting paper.

It is a good idea to press a single type of plant material in each layer. Leave a slip of paper visible with a note of each type and the date it was put in the press.

Press a selection of leaves of different shapes and sizes; fine flower stalks, with some curved and some straight; and curling sweet pea tendrils, which give graceful lines to finish off the sides of a design or add movement.

The best place to store pressed flowers is in the press, but if you do have to remove them, store them in covered, labelled boxes, between layers of tissue paper, in a dry place. The blotting paper can be re-used but should be ironed dry with a warm iron after each batch.

Most flowers can be pressed, with varying degrees of success. Try anything, but discard any which look wrinkled, faded or less than perfect after pressing.

The simplest flowers with single open faces, such as pansies, buttercups, tiny hawthorn blossoms, individual hydrangea florets, pear and cherry blossoms are the easiest to press. Place the flower face down on the blotting paper. Alyssum and cow parsley can be separated into small flower clusters for pressing. These clusters are invaluable as fillers between larger flower-heads, when making pictures. Forget-me-nots will press in small sprays, complete with stalk.

Other single flowers, such as daisies and hellebores, give excellent results, but the domed fleshy centres are difficult to press. To make these lie flat, snip out part of the centre of the flower from the back. Alternatively, for larger flowers, such as the hellebore, press the petals singly and then press the thick centres separately. When dry, slice through the centre and reassemble the flower.

Some flowers disintegrate when pressed flat but will press with the petals folded together facing sideways. Tubular flowers are best pressed in this way. Any flower can be sliced in half to make it lie flatter.

To make a pressed flower picture you will need a picture frame; strong adhesive tape; a coloured backing card or fabric cut to the size of the frame; tweezers; clear-drying glue; a glass-headed pin; a small sharp knife with a fine point; and the pressed plant material.

First, plan your design by drawing it on a piece of paper the same size as the backing card. Don't make the mistake of filling the picture too full. You can follow the curve of an oval frame with a sweep of flowers in one corner only, or build up a central posy shape, leaving the corners empty, or put a trail of flowers across the centre of the frame, or even a complete garland of flowers around the edges with the centre left empty.

Outlines for flower pictures

Lay out the flowers, using tweezers if necessary, on the backing, referring to the pencilled outline. Use the largest flowers towards the centre, decreasing gradually in size towards the outside. Add buds, curved leaves, pieces of fern or tendrils towards the outside to soften the edge. The flowers can be overlapped and small florets used to fill spaces.

When you are happy with the design, lift the edge of the flowers one at a time, place a tiny bead of glue on the back of one petal, and replace in the design. The flowers only need to be held in place lightly, whilst the frame is added. It is the pressure of the frame that holds the flowers eventually.

When all the flowers are in place, cover with the glass and frame. The flowers should be pressed firmly against the glass and the back of the picture frame sealed securely with adhesive tape to prevent moisture from getting in. Pressed flower pictures should be hung out of direct sunlight, which will fade the flowers.

24
Making Pot Pourri

There is nothing nicer than the lingering smell of summer in the middle of winter, which is why so many people buy pot pourri. But it is much pleasanter and cheaper to capture the scents from your own garden with homemade pot pourri.

Pot pourri is a mixture of scented flower petals, fragrant herbs and leaves which are dried and stirred together with a fixative. The fixative is necessary to preserve the fragrance, which would otherwise disappear after a few months.

In summer, collect the petals of such flowers as roses, clove-scented dianthus and carnations, lavender, chamomile, philadelphus (mock orange), elder flowers, freesias, sweet peas, marigolds, sunflowers, peonies—in fact, of any scented flower. Collect the aromatic leaves of pelargoniums, eucalyptus and herbs such as rosemary, lemon balm, lemon verbena, marjoram, peppermint, eau-de-cologne mint, thyme, bay, sage. In spring, gather the petals of narcissi, lily-of-the-valley and wallflowers. Always harvest the plant material during a dry spell, and just as the buds open. Faded flowers will have lost much of their scent.

Drying the petals   All the material must be dried thoroughly. Stretch a layer of net curtain over a frame, spread out one kind of plant material on this and put in a warm, dry room or in an airing cupboard. Alternatively, use a wire cooling rack in a warm room, away from direct sunshine. Turn the petals daily until they are dry and crisp to the touch; this takes about three days in a warm airing cupboard. Herbs can also be hung in bunches in a warm, airy room or airing cupboard. When they are completely dry, strip the leaves from the stems.

If the perfume of the dried petals and herbs is to last, one or more fixatives must be added to the mixture. The more fixatives that are used, the longer the fragrance of the pot pourri will last. Chemists and herbalists sell special fragrant oils which act as fixatives.

Fixatives   The best fixative is orris root, obtainable from a herbalist or chemist. This is the root of *Iris florentina*, and is bought in powdered form. A less satisfactory but cheaper fixative is the root of angelica. After the angelica has flowered, dig it up, dry off the root thoroughly and then grind it to a powder in a liquidiser or electric coffee grinder. An excellent fixative can also be made very simply from the peel of oranges, tangerines or lemons. This has the added bonus of bringing its own tangy perfume to the pot pourri. Peel the fruit very thinly using a potato peeler. Dry the peel in a warm oven for 45 minutes to an hour, until it is crisp. Grind it to a powder as above. Keep the fixatives in air-tight jars in a cool, dark place until needed.

Storing the petals and herbs   Store each kind of dried petal or herb separately, in air-tight jars. Put in 2.5 cm (1 in) of the dried material. Sprinkle with 2.5 ml (½ tsp) coarse salt and 2.5 ml (½ tsp) powdered orris root and/or citrus peel. Repeat the layers until the jar is full. Store the covered jar in the dark to mature for a minimum of three to four weeks.

Mixing the pot pourri   When you have a good selection of prepared herbs and flowers you can mix them together in a pot pourri. The final mixture is a matter of personal choice. You may prefer to use just flower petals, or a mixture of herbs and flowers. Ground spices such as cloves and cinnamon, or ground seeds, such as coriander and fennel, can also be added to a pot pourri. Try different combinations to see which fragrance you find most acceptable. More ingredients can be added later if the scent loses strength; and concentrated oils are available, which can be sprinkled into the pot pourri to strengthen the perfume.

Although there is no 'recipe' for pot pourri as such, I have found these combinations very successful. Use a teacup or coffee mug as a measure.

Rose petal pot pourri: 8 cups rose petals, ½ cup scented pelargonium leaves, 1 cup lemon verbena leaves, 1 cup mock orange blossom, 5 drops rose oil.

Lavender pot pourri: 4 cups stripped lavender flowers, 2 cups rose petals, ½ cup apple mint leaves, ½ cup thyme foliage, ½ cup crushed bay leaves, 5 drops lavender oil.

Springtime pot pourri: 4 cups wallflowers, 2 cups narcissus petals, 1 cup lily-of-the-valley flowers, 2 cups lilac flowers, 5 drops blue lilac oil.

The fragrance of the mixture of pot pourri is best appreciated in open bowls, where it can be stirred and bruised to release the scent. Pot pourri can also be tied in small muslin bags suspended from coathangers or placed in drawers. Or make hanging balls of pot pourri, using a dry foam ball as a base. Spread clear-drying glue over the surface of the ball. Roll it in the pot pourri until the surface of the ball is completely covered. Then wrap the ball in a circle of fine net or lace, tied at the top with ribbon. Pin or glue dried flowers and ribbon loops on the top of the ball to decorate, leaving a long loop to suspend it.

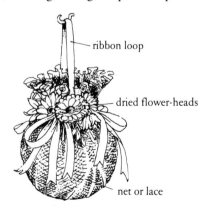

ribbon loop

dried flower-heads

net or lace

A hanging ball of pot pourri

FUN WITH FLOWERS

25
A Christmas Swag

Flower arranging for Christmas is easy. You can't go wrong with a variety of evergreens, some baubles and a scarlet ribbon or two. This year, don't be satisfied with the usual sprig of holly on top of the picture frame. Try this easy-to-make hanging swag of mixed evergreens in oasis, which will stay fresh over the Christmas season. This arrangement can be suspended above a picture or from the same nail as the picture so that it rests on the picture frame, over an alcove or over the top of a doorway.

Branches of conifers or cedars, particularly those with a blue tinge, or branches cut from the base of the Christmas tree, are a good contrast in texture with the shiny surface of holly. The use of variegated holly or variegated ivy with evergreens is good to lighten their otherwise rather dense colour.

The base of the swag is made from soaked oasis and chicken

wire. After the greenery has died, save the base. Although it will dry out and cannot be used again for fresh plant material, it will be useful for dried or glycerined arrangements.

You will need:

Foliage – *Cedrus atlantica* 'Glauca' (blue cedar); *Juniperus squamata* 'Blue Carpet'; *Ilex* (holly); *Ilex aquifolium* 'Aureo-marginata' (variegated holly); *Hedera helix* 'Glacier' (ivy).

Mechanics – Large block of oasis; cling film; chicken wire; reel wire or cord for hanging; three red glass baubles; red satin ribbon.

The base and background of conifer

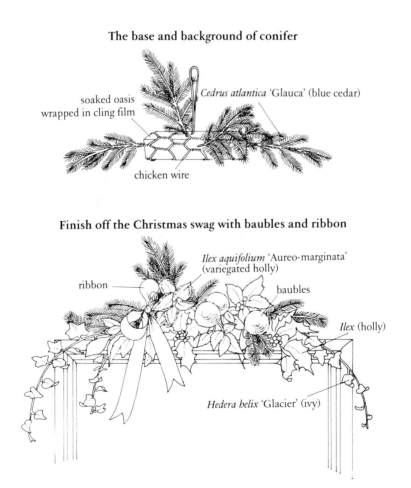

soaked oasis wrapped in cling film

Cedrus atlantica 'Glauca' (blue cedar)

chicken wire

Finish off the Christmas swag with baubles and ribbon

Ilex aquifolium 'Aureo-marginata' (variegated holly)

ribbon

baubles

Ilex (holly)

Hedera helix 'Glacier' (ivy)

Cut a large block of oasis in half along its length. Soak it thoroughly and wrap it completely in cling film. Cut a piece of chicken wire to wrap right around the block, with a small overlap at the top and sides. Bend the ends of the mesh together to secure it. Add a short hanging loop of wire or cord in the middle of one long side, which is not seen in the finished swag.

To assemble the swag, insert a branch of conifer to the left of centre into the top of the oasis, piercing the cling film. Add a curving branch to each side and short sprays to the front and the base, to complete an asymmetrical triangle. If you have difficulty piercing the film with some of the thicker branches, make a hole first with a skewer.

Intersperse the conifer with short, feathery tips of juniper. Add sprays of holly following inside the outline formed by the conifer. Add a long trail of ivy at each side and shorter trails off centre and to the front.

Wire the baubles to a bare stem of holly and insert, grouped to the right of the design. Make a satin bow and cut the ribbon ends into forks. Thread a length of wire through the back of the bow, twist the ends together and place the bow to the left of the design.

A hanging swag is also ideal for a wedding arrangement. If the base is made to hang the other way up, that is with the short end to the top, it can be suspended over a pew end by a loop of white satin ribbon. Use light green foliage as the background and choose flowers to tie in with the wedding colour scheme.

26
A Christmas Flower Arrangement

Red carnations are traditional Christmas flowers. They combine very well with evergreens and are long lasting. To give more interest to a Christmas arrangement, add a figure or a robin. Anything other than plant material which forms part of a flower arrangement is known in floral art terms as an accessory. Accessories should be an integral part of a design, not added as an afterthought. They are used to provide interest, but should not dominate the display. The robin in this design brings a different dimension to the group and if it is taken away the arrangement loses its vitality. It is a good example of how to use an accessory. It ties in with the brown of the base and the red of the flowers, and it also echoes the earthy note given by the driftwood. Cover it up in the photograph in the colour section and something more than the robin is lost from the arrangement.

The large piece of driftwood has been permanently fixed to a base by means of a screw coming through from the underside of the board (see page 54).

You will need:

Foliage – *Ilex aquifolium* 'Aureo-marginata' (variegated holly); *Hedera canariensis* 'Variegata' (variegated ivy); *Skimmia japonica*; eucalyptus.

Flowers – Red long-stemmed carnations; red spray carnations.

Mechanics – Driftwood supported on a base; large hessian-covered base; robin; oasis; florist's tape; bulb bowl.

Position the driftwood on its base to the right on the main base. Perch the robin at the foot of the driftwood to the right and slightly to the back. Tape the oasis securely inside the bowl and position it at the foot of the driftwood and to the left.

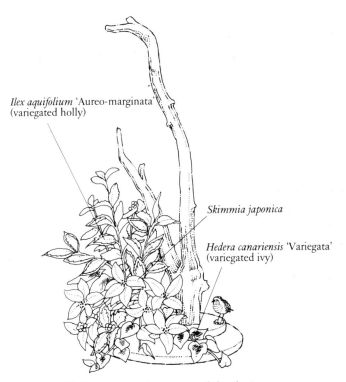

Ilex aquifolium 'Aureo-marginata'
(variegated holly)

Skimmia japonica

Hedera canariensis 'Variegata'
(variegated ivy)

Add skimmia to the centre of the design

Insert branches of holly to the back and sides to give a loosely triangular shape. Fill in to the front and sides with the variegated ivy, bringing trails of ivy over the edge of the base. Add skimmia to the centre and back to give depth to the design.

Place the long-stemmed carnations following the outline of the triangle. Shorten some of the stems to recess some flowers and place others to come forward at the front. Intersperse the spray carnations throughout the design and soften with eucalyptus. (See the colour section.)

27
Outdoor Flower
Arrangements

Flower arrangements are not usually necessary out of doors. However, on a special occasion, such as a wedding or garden party, a floral display could be placed at a gateway or entrance, out of the wind, or in a sheltered porch. A large scale arrangement is needed out of doors and if a pedestal would look out of place, an imitation bay tree will harmonise with most surroundings. These 'trees' look most effective arranged in pairs, one each side of the doorway or entrance.

'Bay trees' are fun to make and the foundation can be used over and over for any type of arrangement. Try a Christmas display of holly with tips of fir branches and red ribbons; an autumnal mixture of dried flowers and glycerined leaves; or a fresh midsummer arrangement of bay leaves and spray chrysanthemums with green and white ribbons.

To make the foundation tree you will need: an inner flower pot 18 cm (7 in) in diameter; an attractive outer pot 25 cm (10 in) in diameter; ready-to-mix sand and cement; a straight thick branch 1.2 m (4 ft) long; an oasis ball 20 cm (8 in) in diameter; florist's tape; cling film; satin ribbon; coloured pebbles.

Cut the side shoots off a well-shaped branch to form the trunk of the tree and cut it to the measurement given.

Make a firm paste of the sand-and-cement and water. Wedge the branch between a few stones so that it stands in the centre of the smaller pot. Fill up the pot with the cement and leave to set for 24 hours. (The reason for using two pots is that when the tree needs to be transported, it will weigh less if it is permanently fixed to a fairly small pot. The larger outer pot is needed for stability and to make the tree look balanced and not top heavy. The outer pot can also be changed to suit the occasion.)

Soak the oasis and push it down on the top of the branch. Wind tape around the ball to secure it, then wrap in cling film to help retain the moisture. Put the pot in the larger ornamental container. Place in its final position. Fill the container with coloured pebbles to hide the inner pot and give weight to the base.

For a Christmas flower-ball, use holly, cupressus, variegated ivy, red single-flower carnations and red florist's ribbon. The diameter of the finished ball should be about 40 cm (16 in). Cut

Creating the outline with holly

Finish off the 'bay tree' with ribbon

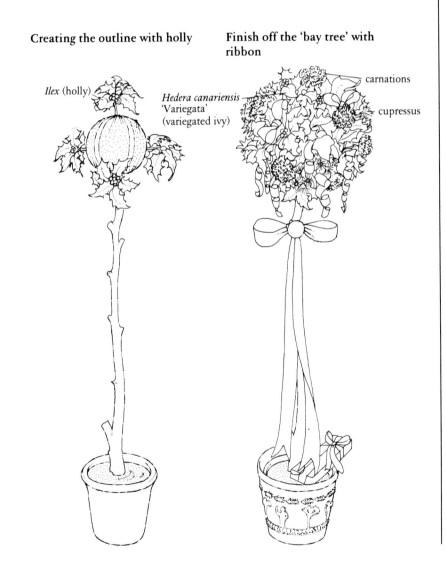

Ilex (holly)

Hedera canariensis 'Variegata' (variegated ivy)

carnations

cupressus

four sprigs of holly and insert them into the oasis to the top, bottom and sides of the ball to give an outline about this size.

Use these four placements as an outline guide to fill in a background of foliage, keeping a fairly even ball shape. Add single leaves of the ivy to lighten the dense green of the holly. Add the flowers, evenly spaced over the ball.

Make ribbon curls by drawing narrow florist's ribbon across the blade of a knife, then wire and add to the arrangement. Add a bow of ribbon below the flowers, leaving long streamers.

A pretty, summery flower-ball tree can be made with bay or skimmia, golden privet, alchemilla and yellow chrysanthemums. Use a wicker basket for the outer container, and finish with yellow ribbon curls and bows.

28
An Apple-head
Flower Seller

Dried flowers are sometimes difficult to display effectively, particularly the smallest blooms, which get lost amongst glycerined foliage and flowers. Here is one way to display clusters of tiny dried flowers and the smaller everlastings. Create this delightful flower seller complete with her baskets of blooms. Her wizened old features are made from an apple.

An apple-head flower seller

This is really an excuse for me to include my favourite hobby of making apple-head dolls in this book! Apple-head carving is an old craft which reputedly originated with the North American Indians, who dried the apples in the sun. In this country it is quicker to use the oven. Of all the things I have made I have enjoyed creating these the most. You don't have to make the heads into flower sellers; they can be gardeners, sailors, washerwomen and drunkards, according to how you dress them. But for this book they have to be flower sellers.

The peeled apple is sculpted into a face, and as the fruit dries it shrivels into wrinkles and becomes soft and pliable. At this stage, the face can be moulded to give different expressions, before completing the drying process. Make-up, eyes and hair are added. The apple eventually dries quite hard and is coated with clear spray varnish to make it permanent. Although the apple-heads last indefinitely, they should be kept in a dry place, or they may absorb moisture from the atmosphere and darken in colour.

Making the face To make the head you will need: unblemished golden or red delicious apple, which shrinks well; lemon juice; salt; sharp kitchen knife or scalpel; apple corer; pipe cleaners; pastry brush; large white glass-headed pins or small, white beads for the eyes; black paint; scrap of lambswool, mohair wool or long pile white or grey fur for the hair; silica gel; flesh tinted make-up; red nail polish; powder blusher; adhesive; artist's clear picture varnish or similar acrylic spray.

Peel the apple very thinly. Decide which is the flattest side of the apple to make into the face and with the point of a pin lightly score the face into three sections: forehead, nose area and chin.

To cut the temples and the bulge of the cheeks at each side of the apple (looking at it 'face-on'), cut down from the top, about 6 mm (¼ in) from the side to the first line (a). Remove wedges of apple by making a slanting cut upwards from just below the scored line (a).

Into the front of the face, make a vertical cut down from the top, about 6 mm (¼ in), until this cut meets line (a). Remove this section of apple with a slanting cut upwards from line (b).

Cut into the apple on line (b) to a depth of about 6 mm (¼ in). Then cut upwards from the base of the apple to form the mouth and chin area and to complete the nose shape. Make the sides of the nose with two slanting cuts running down from (a) to (b) about 6 mm (¼ in) deep. Remove a tiny wedge of apple on these cuts.

Cut away the curve of the apple each side of the chin area to define the jaw. Shape in the back of the head by removing a thin

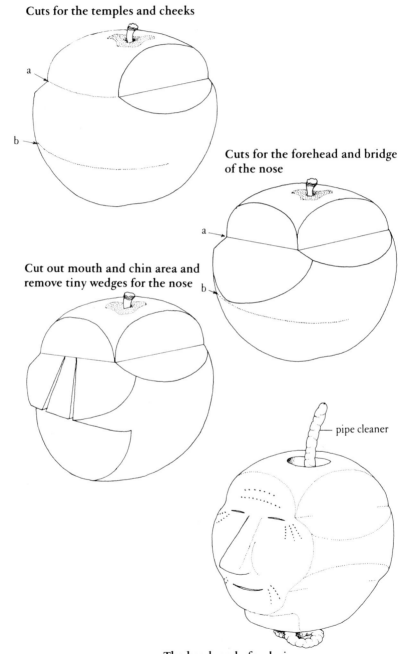

Cuts for the temples and cheeks

a

b

Cuts for the forehead and bridge
of the nose

a

b

Cut out mouth and chin area and
remove tiny wedges for the nose

b

pipe cleaner

The head ready for drying

slice of apple about half way down the back, sloping inwards at the neck.

Using the tip of a knife, scrape very gently over the face to smooth the sharp edges of the features. Using a pastry brush, brush over the entire head with lemon juice and then with salt to prevent discoloration.

Make a slit each side of the nose on line (a) about 6 mm (¼ in) in, for the eyes. Do not remove a wedge of apple for the eye socket as the slit opens up during the drying process. Make a shallow, curved slit into the apple below the nose for the mouth.

Using a pin, lightly score lines, which will form wrinkles when the apple dries, on the forehead and the outer edges of the mouth and eyes. Carefully remove the core, using an apple corer.

Sprinkle salt liberally over the head. Brush over with more lemon juice until the salt is completely dissolved. Pass a pipe cleaner through the hole at the centre of the apple. Make a twist in the pipe cleaner below the base for the apple to rest on.

Drying the apple-head (1st stage)   Suspend the apple-head from the oven shelf with the pipe cleaner. Set the oven to the lowest temperature and dry for 24–30 hours, or until it has shrunk to about the size of a golf ball. It will no longer be sticky, but pliable and soft. At this stage, it is easy to mould the features and wrinkles into the expressions you want. Squash the head from the top to make it smile or emphasise the downward wrinkles with a pin to make it miserable. You can also chip away small slivers of apple to make the features more pronounced. Brush the whole head with skin-tone liquid make-up, brushing it into all the crevices.

Drying the apple-head (2nd stage)   Completely immerse the head in silica gel (see page 63) in an airtight container, filling the hollow core with the crystals. Leave undisturbed for two days, when the head will be quite dry but still soft to the touch. Brush off the crystals. Alternatively leave the head in a warm airing cupboard for at least a week.

To make the hands is easy. Cut very thin strips of apple. Dry and colour them as for the head (the drying time will be shorter), and trim them into hands and fingers after the first drying process is complete. Shape the hands as you want them and then finish drying.

To complete the head, insert a bead or pin into each eye socket and with the tip of a very fine brush dab black paint on the centre for the pupil. Use red nail polish to colour the mouth and powder blusher for the cheeks. When you are satisfied with the features, spray the entire head with clear, quick-drying varnish.

Smooth short lengths of wool or fur over the top of the head and twist them into a bun at the back. When you are satisfied with the hair style, remove the hair, spread glue over the top of the head and fix the hair in place. Pins can also be used to secure the ends of the hair: push them well into the apple.

To dress the flower seller, you will need: a cardboard cone (the inside of a wool cone is ideal); dress fabric with a small pattern; matching narrow ribbon; scraps of lace; scrap of old jersey or sock to make a shawl; sewing thread; glue; small baskets filled with dried flowers.

Cover the cone by wrapping it in a quarter-circle of fabric, turning the ends under the base. Glue or stitch the fabric in place. Cut a strip of fabric 15 × 40 cm (6 × 16 in) for the skirt. Join the two short sides and finish one long edge with narrow lace. Gather the other edge, slip the skirt over the cone and pull to fit the waist. Tie in place with a sash of ribbon, covering the raw edges and leaving a bow at the back.

Spread glue over the point of the cone and press the head down onto the cone. Push a pin through the back of the head and cone together, where it will not be seen, to hold it firmly.

To make the arms and sleeves, bend the tips at each end of a medium-gauge florist's wire. Wrap the whole wire in cotton wool and bind with thread. Cover with a piece of nylon stocking and stitch in place. Cut a strip of fabric 15 × 25 cm

(6 × 10 in). Neaten the short ends with narrow lace. Fold the strip in half lengthwise and stitch to form a tube. Insert the covered wire into the sleeves. Glue the apple hands to the ends of the arms and tie in the fabric with ribbon at the wrists to cover the join. Centre the arms at the back of the neck and stitch the fabric to the dress at the shoulders and back neck. Bend the arms forward. Add a lace collar and a knitted shawl.

Set the flower seller on a hessian-covered base with small baskets of dried flowers.

29
Frozen Flowers

How lovely, in the middle of winter, to be able to appreciate the full beauty of a rose picked from the garden at the height of the summer. Wouldn't it be wonderful to capture those fleeting flowers, like morning glory and hibiscus, which bloom and fade in one day and to be able to admire them for more than their allotted 24 hours?

Well, you can. Freeze flowers in water to create a rose bowl or an ice bucket. The flower heads shine through the ice walls which, in artificial lighting, give the appearance of a very expensive ceramic container.

The bowl can be used to serve ice cream or sorbet at a party and the bucket will hold ice cubes. Both can be on display for an hour or more, depending on the thickness of the ice walls, until they show signs of melting. They can then be returned to the freezer to harden up for another occasion.

To make the rose bowl you will need: a large glass bowl and a second bowl, which is at least 6 cm (2½ in) less in diameter. The smaller bowl must fit inside the larger one, leaving a gap between the two of at least 3 cm (1¼ in) all around. You will also need clear tape, tweezers, a sharp knife and a selection of small roses, buds, flower-heads and leaves.

To make an ice bucket, choose two plastic seaside buckets of different sizes which have the same 3 cm (1¼ in) gap between them when fitted one inside the other. Use a selection of geranium florets, ivy leaves and small flower-heads for the plant material.

The bowl and the ice bucket are made in the same way. Place a pattern of flowers and leaves in the base. Use adhesive tape to suspend the small bowl inside the larger one, leaving approximately 3 cm (1¼ in) clearance at the base.

Using tweezers and the point of a knife, position flower-heads round the sides of the bowl at the base, with the faces of the flowers against the glass sides of the outer bowl. Add flowers to a depth of 5 cm (2 in). Gently pour water over the flowers to cover them, without disturbing the arrangement. Freeze until solid, preferably overnight.

Add a second border of flowers and leaves in the same way, to fill the bowl almost to the top. Place a border of flowers, with their faces turned upwards, at the top. Fill with water as before and freeze until solid.

To remove the ice container dip the outer bowl in very hot water for a few seconds to loosen it. Pour hot water into the inner bowl and it will come out easily.

If the ice bowl becomes opaque after storing in the freezer, wipe it with the palm of the hand to clear the ice and allow the flowers to be seen.

A rose bowl and ice bucket

Index

94